Faces of Feminism

Pamela Harris

To my parents
and my daughters
with love and with hope

FACES OF FEMINISM

PORTRAITS OF WOMEN ACROSS CANADA

by

PAMELA HARRIS

WITH WORDS BY THE
WOMEN PORTRAYED

SECOND
STORY
Press

CANADIAN CATALOGUING IN PUBLICATION DATA

Harris, Pamela, 1940 -
Faces of feminism: a photo documentation

Some text in French.
ISBN 0-929005-37-6 (bound)
ISBN 0-929005-36-8 (pbk.)

1. Feminists - Canada - Portraits.
2. Feminism - Canada.   I.Title

TR681.W6H37 1992   779'.930542'0971   C92-094979-7

Printed in duotone on Paralux paper by Herzig Somerville Limited, Toronto
Printed and Bound in Canada

Faces of Feminism has been published with the support of
The Canadian Research Institute For The Advancement of Women

Second Story Press gratefully acknowledges the assistance of the
Ontario Arts Council, Multicultural and Citizenship Canada and the Canada Council

Published by
SECOND STORY PRESS
760 Bathurst St.
Toronto, Ontario
M5S 2R6

CONTENTS

ACKNOWLEDGMENTS

Faces of Feminism has had a long history. Many people lent a hand along the way.

Primary funding for the *Faces of Feminism* project came from The Canada Council and The Ontario Arts Council. The Toronto Photographers Workshop gave initial impetus and support. They also exhibited and toured the final collection, on which this book is based. The Canadian Research Institute for the Advancement of Women awarded a research grant. As co-publisher they facilitated the publication of *Faces of Feminism* and oversaw donations. The Toronto Arts Council aided my writing. The National Archives of Canada added a substantial number of the images to their collection. I am grateful to all of these institutions for their support and encouragement.

Throughout this project I was greatly helped by my husband, Randall McLeod. He critiqued my writing, helped with translations, introduced me to computers and, most important, provided support and patience over the long haul. Our daughters, Katy and Emily, have lived with *Faces of Feminism* for a good part of their lives, finding it a source of interesting experiences, some annoyance, and a widening view of women's lives.

Angela Miles, friend for two and a half decades, played an important role in *Faces of Feminism,* imprinting it with her knowledge and abiding optimism about the grass-roots women's movement. Gail Geltner offered wry humour and steady engagement. While I was preparing the book, Arlene Moscovitch and Vandra Masemann provided warmth and editorial suggestions; Melissa Rombout gave good council; Brian MacLeod Rogers added contract advice; Marian Smith advised on fundraising, and Maia Sutnik helped to edit and sequence the images. Ernie Herzig and Hendrick Rens carefully attended us through the printing process.

Gary Hall, director of the Toronto Photographers Workshop furthered *Faces of Feminism* throughout its history. The Workshop's program-director, Kim Fullerton, organized the exhibition and tour and produced a catalogue.

This book would not have been published without the commitment of Second Story Press: Lois Pike, Margie Wolfe and especially Liz Martin. She made the case for a risky undertaking and put innumerable hours into each phase of production, always retaining her equanimity.

From its inception, *Faces of Feminism* has been dependent on the assistance of women across Canada, some of whom also became friends. Of those who helped and advised me, I can name here only a few (in chronological order of provinces visited):

When I began the project in Toronto in 1984, Lynne Fernie, Frieda Forman and Mary O'Brien were particularly helpful. Julie Nasmith and Marion Neglia pitched in for the exhibition. As I began to research the women's movement across Canada, Diane Duggan, Shelley Finson, Pat Israel, Kay Macpherson, Greta Hofmann Nemiroff, Barbara Roberts and Jill McCalla Vickers gave me a wealth of suggestions. Pat Kipping got me organized in Nova Scotia (1985) along with Muriel Duckworth and Joella Foulds. Jane Morrigan and Marie Welton looked after me. Mary Sparling exhibited the Nova Scotia work in 1987. In Manitoba (1985) Dinah Ceplis, Sharon Zenith Corne, Janine Gibson, Judy Marchand and Marian Yeo were tremendously supportive. (And in 1991, Chris Clark and Marian Yeo sparked the fundraising effort for this book with their example of women-getting-things-done.) In Saskatchewan (1986) Nancy Poole gave invaluable assistance; Bonnie Johnson, Mona Frederickson Katawne and Priscilla Settee took care of me; Georgie Taylor gave advice.

In Newfoundland (1986) Ann Bell was greatly generous with information and aid. Marie Newhook, Anne Power and Wendy Williams put me up. Dorothy Inglis was an important first contact. In New Brunswick (1986) Corinne Gallant, Madeleine Le Blanc and Rosella Melanson gave direction and help; Shirley Bear welcomed our whole family into her community. That same summer, Jill Lightwood and Beth Percival were helpful contacts on Prince Edward Island. Of the British Columbia women who contributed to my research in 1988 I must especially mention Jan Barnsley, Gloria Greenfield, Jillian Ridington, Esther Shannon and Betsy Warland. Linda Denning made me her guest and friend, as did Marcia Braundy. In Alberta (1988) I was advised by Sara Berger, Rebecca Coulter and the Newsmagazine Collective. Trudy Richardson took me in. In Quebec (1986 and 1989) Micheline de Sève and Lise Moisan were key advisers. Janick Belleau, Lanie

Melamud and Ruth Selwyn also sent a wealth of suggestions. On my several visits, Judith Crawley, along with Bev and George Torok, made me feel at home.

There were many others. In addition, there were the women who invited me in to make a portrait, wrote a text to accompany that image and yet for reasons of space and editing are not in the book. All are part of *Faces of Feminism* and to all I owe a debt of gratitude.

℘

Finally, there is a most important group, which it is a great pleasure to acknowledge. These are the people who made it possible for the project entitled *Faces of Feminism* to become this book: our publication sponsors and our two major donors.

The names of our publication sponsors appear at the end of the book. Answering our appeal, these hundreds of people bought in advance a book that was only a promise, so that this publication could be a reality. Their support, flowing in from around the country and beyond, gave us tremendous encouragement and created the momentum to carry us through.

Yet for all our fundraising efforts we still came up short until one of the women in the project heard of our situation and volunteered to help. This was Nancy Jackman. She found for us an anonymous donor of great generosity and added equally generous support of her own. With a flourish, these two beneficent women finished the job begun by our publication sponsors, and *Faces of Feminism* could go to the printer.

All of this support, financial but also emotional, has been a great gift.

To everyone, friend and stranger, who supported
Faces of Feminism, a heartfelt THANK YOU.

— *Pamela Harris*

PREFACE

Lisa Steele

AS WE NEAR THE TURN to the twenty-first century, specifics of the lives of women continue to surface with all their depth and complexity. Pamela Harris' project *Faces of Feminism* issues directly from this well of female diversity.

Between 1984 and 1989 Pamela Harris researched the grass-roots women's movement in Canada, photographing women across the country and inviting each to provide a written text to accompany her image. The result is a collaboration between Harris and the women she photographed.

The poems, stories, anecdotes and analyses that accompany the portraits are as varied as the subjects themselves. Harris' sampling of what-it-is-to-be-a-woman includes old, young, at home, in the work place, on the land, hurt but recovered, whole-perfectly-whole, proud, banded together and defiantly singular women.

The photographs have great presence and draw us in. Harris has a way of making portraits that allows content to pour into the isolated frame. By heightening the narrative qualities of the photographs, she increases the viewer's desire to look inside, to get to know these women, to engage.

Few of those photographed are household names. What unites them is their sense of engagement. Their writings make reference to the personal decisions and collective struggles that have contributed to each woman's feminist identity. Having constructed self-identities that allow dignity and action, the women in *Faces of Feminism* become — in all their ordinariness — role models. To use the words of Lucy Lippard, this is "poetry that talks back, that would act as part of the world, not simply as a mirror of it."

When work from *Faces of Feminism* was exhibited across Canada, many people responded with the wish that the material could be a book. That it has become one is a fact we can all celebrate.

REGARDING FEMINISM

Angela Miles

IN *Faces of Feminism* Pamela Harris presents the words and images of women who are consciously engaged in making history, acting collectively while remaining robustly themselves. The opportunity to meet these women is a welcome one. For they, along with many thousands of others across Canada, are part of a complex movement whose real face is too rarely seen. Pamela Harris' photographs and the writings that accompany them document the spirit and variety that animate feminism — a global movement that is transforming the way women and men understand and live in the world.

Feminism is the sum of rich and varied initiatives by diverse women in private and in public, working to change human society. There are a multitude of feminist organizations, but it is not membership in these that determines whether one is part of the women's movement. What makes a woman a feminist is identification with women and commitment to women's aspirations and issues. The impact feminism has had is the result of countless individual actions and an enormous range of collective practice.

Today, women in Kenya are greening the desert with millions of trees. Thousands of street traders in India are campaigning for their rights through their Self-Employed Women's Association. Canadian, San Salvadoran and South African women are raising their voices in the constitutional processes of their countries. Women are camping in protest outside the nuclear air base at Greenham Common in England. They are networking against the external debt in Latin America and the Caribbean. Women everywhere are resisting violence against women — in all its forms — including the misogyny inherent in many religious fundamentalisms. Women are working in Europe and the Pacific to end sex tourism, combating incest in North America, resisting dowry deaths in India, opposing the laws of Sharia in Pakistan, challenging the prohibition of birth-control and abortion in Ireland, organizing and educating against clitoridectomy in Africa. All these campaigns are part of a movement that is increasingly global. Around the world, feminists are making the deeply radical claim that women's rights are human rights.

Feminism is not monolithic of course. Not all feminists agree; priorities vary as do analyses and approaches; debate waxes hot and heavy around many issues. Women's struggles vary with context, and even within the same context feminists often disagree. Here in Canada, some feminists place hope in legal reforms and electoral power of which others despair. Some see the main task as educating women to enter the sciences, while others are more concerned to transform science. Feminist activism takes many forms. Feminists participate in public education, personal change, direct action, the creation of alternative institutions, mass campaigns and/or the provision of support and services for women. They may emphasize the spiritual or the material aspects of struggle. They may give priority to achieving autonomy, or to building coalitions, or both. This diversity of practice is increasing, and feminism is enriched and deepened, as more — and more varied — groups of women find their voices.

In the decades since the women's movement re-emerged in North America, there has never been a time when the "death of feminism" was not discussed, predicted, bemoaned or celebrated. This litany of feminism's doom partly reflects a political agenda to deny women's challenges to existing social structures. It also reflects a failure to understand and recognize the new and highly varied political forms that feminism is taking. For feminism is not a game of catch-up or a bid to reverse the power relations between men and women. Feminists are concerned not only to gain equal access to social structures, but also to transform them. We want to redefine what it means to be human as well as to achieve human status for women, to change power as well as to win it.

This transformative potential is implicit in all feminist activity, whether or not it is articulated. For even the most modest of feminist demands are unthinkable without major structural changes. Although it is now theoretically conceivable for an individual woman to go into male-dominated institutions on equal terms with men, women as a group cannot be included equally in institutions which are built on our subordination unless there is qualitative change to those institutions. At the most basic level, pressure for women's equal inclusion in the labour force necessarily throws into question the relationship between home and work place and requires the recognition and reorganization of unpaid reproductive work and responsibility. Pay equity will require not merely women's access to better-paying men's jobs but increased status, pay and power for women's traditionally undervalued work, both the currently underpaid and the unpaid labour. This challenges both the hierarchical structure and the underlying principles of the work force.

Even those issues that seem most narrowly focused on women's inclusion in existing structures contain implicit, if not explicit, challenges to those structures. Equality for women in health care, for example, is not simply about more women becoming doctors but about increasing the power of other health-care workers and patients and making the currently under-resourced work of care and healing the defining centre of the system. Ending men's monopoly on spiritual leadership contributes to more equal, people-centred and communal religious institutions, not just to women's equality. The depth and intensity of resistance to women's seemingly elementary demands for simple "fairness" is testimony to the far-reaching transformative consequences of these demands.

In our competitive, individualistic and profit-centred society, where means are presumed to be separable from ends and subordinate to them, the dominant culture constructs the world as a series of unequal and exclusive oppositions. Women and women's work of creating and sustaining life are associated with the less valued (even dangerous) side of the dichotomies. The personal is opposed to the political and the private to the public. In each case the former (traditionally female) realm is seen as potentially subversive of the important concerns of the latter (male) realm. In this schizophrenic construction of the world, emotion and reason are perceived as contradictory capacities, with emotion a potential threat to privileged reason. The demands of body are presumed to conflict with those of mind, and the spirit is seen to be in constant danger of corruption by the flesh. Society is valued over the natural, the individual over community, and each pair is understood to be in perennial tension. Independence is thought to be compromised by connection, diversity to preclude commonality, differences to necessitate inequality.

The affirmation of women and of women's concerns and interests that lies at the core of feminism runs absolutely counter to this dualistic world view and its underlying instrumental values. For instance, a basic tenet of feminism is that "the personal is political." Far from being outside of politics, private life and personal relationships institutionalize power and are shaped by it. Marriage, the family, motherhood, love, sexuality — all are political institutions. Similarly, rape, prostitution, abortion, wife-beating and incest must be understood politically. But to say that "the personal is political" is not merely to recognize that private life is structured by patriarchal power. It also expresses a conviction that the female-associated values such as caring, nurture, love and co-operation — which currently are relegated to and distorted within the limits of private life — should be the shaping principles of the whole community.

Universalizing these connective values is essential in order to heal the fragmentation of our world. And this integration is both the means and end of feminist practice as we attempt to prefigure in our work the values we seek in the future. Feminism requires that we aspire now, as well as in our visions for the future, to relationships in which reason and emotion are complementary capacities and in which both commonality and diversity are celebrated.

In a world organized around people rather than the requirements of profit, the needs of individual and community would not be in opposition but would enrich and strengthen each other. People could live in peaceful coexistence with nature and with each other. Such a vision has relevance for the whole of society, not only for women. This radical challenge to race and class as well as gender oppression is a product of many and varied women's voices, especially those of women subject to multiple forms of domination.

Each woman's articulation of her identity as a woman and recognition of shared female interests and experiences provides the basis for her participation in the women's movement. However, this women-identification also provides the frame within which she can discover her particular connections with women of her own community and, hence, explore her differences from other women. This awareness in turn provides her a place to stand in the general dialogue. Thus, for feminists, affirming women's similarities goes hand in hand with affirming our differences. Each supports the other. They are part of the same process.

Feminism's difficult — but ultimately liberating — challenge is to build sisterhood across differences, using the differences as resources in developing shared critiques and visions. To do this, feminists need to construct specific identities as places to reach out from rather than hide behind. We need to challenge and criticize as well as respect and support each other. This dynamic process is central to the continuing creation and re-creation of feminism as a multi-centred and open-ended movement. There is no "typical" feminist and no set dogma. This is a movement in which myriad issues and concerns enrich rather than displace common struggle.

Faces of Feminism is eloquent testimony to the vitality of the women's movement in Canada. Like feminism itself, this book is about sisterhood within diversity, about solidarity without homogeneity. In recording a politics grounded in daily life, Pamela Harris celebrates the largely unsung courage, creativity and commitment women bring to both their politics and their daily life. The pictures and text that follow chronicle women affirming themselves and one another as they challenge the status quo and work to create a world which honours women and preserves life. These women — farming, organizing, doing research, making music, practising law, resisting violence, raising children, providing health care — are part of a global movement that is bringing hope to the world as well as to women.

PORTRAITS

AND

WORDS

MAXINE TYNES

Poet; Dartmouth, Nova Scotia

women
we keepers and sharers of ancient secrets
of loving
and making homes of houses
of loving
and making love
of loving
and making life
of loving
and making our men whole
of loving
and being women, wives, mothers, sisters, daughters, lovers,
strong, aunts, free, grandmothers, constant, nieces,
women, and Black
we women of colour
distant daughters of
the Nile, the Sahara, Kenya, Zaire, Sudan
the Serengeti
we dance the body-music of light and shadow
we share the palette spectrum
the obsidian sunshade
burnished blue-black brown tantan sepia
coffeecoffee cream ebony
delight of womanskin
strong in
alive in
free in
loving in
working in
laughing in
sharing in
mothering in
growing in
aging in
this skin
this night shade of many shades
this womanskin
we women
keepers and sharers of ancient secrets

JANE MORRIGAN

Dairy Farmer; Scotsburn, Nova Scotia

I FARM FOR A LIVING, and I do it for the pleasure of friendship with these Jersey cows and for the love of hard work on the land. Working with animals and operating this farm are, to me, equal to anything a person could do. I love the cows, and I believe they love me, too, in their own way. I am grateful for knowing them, for the rich communication of body movement, eye contact and sound. I have watched them from birth to old age — mothers, daughters and granddaughters in the herd. Farming by myself means that I can tune in totally to the animals and the farm, without distraction or compromise.

I wish more women would see farming as one viable alternative to traditional occupations. Granted, opportunities for any individual to enter farming are rapidly diminishing, and certainly the economics of Canadian farming are grim. But it is a myth that farm work is too physically demanding for a woman to do. The fact is that there are many men who are hard put to keep up with me in a day's work, and I am simply a woman of average size who is strong from vigorous, hard work over many years.

There is a terrible imbalance in agriculture in that men own most of the land and control most of the industry in Canada. Since men dominate agriculture, so do practices and policies characterized by male socialization: competitiveness, obsession with efficiency, subjugation of land and animals, and, generally, very little compassion. There was a time in history when women were the farmers. In our rich part of the world the pendulum has now swung completely the other way. Something in between would satisfy me, since I believe that balance is the basis of a healthy world.

PERSIMMON BLACKBRIDGE

Artist; Vancouver, British Columbia

I STARTED DOING ARTWORK at the same time and for the same reasons that I became a feminist — out of desperation. Desperation still drives my work. It's a good enough engine. Sometimes my work is directly political, and sometimes the politics are spoken only in the loud language of bodies — women's bodies. I make pieces that combine images and text and are about specific friends of mine and what the system has done to them. I let the viewer make the generalizations.

Sheila Gilhooly and I made *Still Sane*, a combination of text and sculpture about the three years Sheila spent in mental hospitals for being a lesbian. After *Still Sane* came out as a book, Geri Ferguson asked me if I wanted to do some artwork about prisons with her. Geri has spent most of her life going in and out of prison. So we started working on *Doing Time*, which ended up including three other ex-prisoners. It's very beautiful and very raw at the same time. Here's part of what Geri has to say:

"In prison, time is your worst enemy. Parts of my life feel like I've been unconscious for years. I learnt how to close up and pretend I never saw another woman's pain. I have lain awake all night in prison trying to tell myself I will recover when they let me out, but maybe I won't. I can't breathe in here. The air is always smoky, and it smells of years of decaying flesh. What kind of a person am I to survive this?"

DARLENE BIRCH

Midwife; St. Eustache, Manitoba

THE MOST DIRECT INFLUENCES on my desire to become a midwife were my sense of what it is to be female and the positive births of my first three children. I rejoice in being a woman, in the sisterhood that gives my life substance. I work for women; I work with women, and the exchange of love and trust with these women makes my work possible and in turn results from my work.

I'm not an activist in the large sense of the word. The changes that I facilitate stem from my own experience of childbirth, my own convictions. Our abilities and the qualities we bring to help a birthing woman are ultimately rooted in our own personal history.

There was a woman whom I admired very much who illustrated this well. Alice was a native Ojibwe woman of about seventy years of age. Many babies had been born into her hands. I had the privilege of attending a birth with her a number of years ago. As we sat and drank tea with the labouring woman, watching as she rocked and walked, Alice did not speak of the numbers of babies she'd caught or of the variations of labour and birth. Rather she spoke shyly of the birth of her own first child.

This manner of passing on information and influence is in itself womanly — acting from internal knowledge without fear of being subjective. As I support a woman, one-to-one, she will in turn support another, and the connection will grow and be very strong. Many women whom I've helped are now aspiring midwives. Our power lies in our communities first.

The current reclaiming of reproductive rights was inevitable since the way in which we deal with reproduction is an essential component of our female sexuality and therefore of ourselves. I strive to help women feel the power and fullness of their individual childbearing.

THE SOUTH ASIAN WOMEN'S COMMUNITY CENTRE

Montreal, Quebec

THE SOUTH ASIAN WOMEN'S COMMUNITY CENTRE came into being to help women come out of their isolation to a place where language was no barrier, where roots were shared, where no explanations were required about dress and language and our way of life.

SACC is an egalitarian organization founded by women for women. We come from India, Pakistan, Nepal, Sri Lanka, Bangladesh, and Bhutan — refugees, housewives, professionals, factory workers, businesswomen, students — but when we come together at the Centre we are there as women. Because the affairs at the Centre are conducted entirely by women, we have many success stories to tell of our own inner growth and the realization of ourselves as equals in our world.

Through various activities SACC brings women out of their homes to the Centre. One activity that has proved very successful is the monthly potluck lunch, with talks on subjects such as rental issues, daycare, immigration and health care, to name a few. The talks are followed by discussions which everyone is encouraged to join. Over the years, these discussions have become increasingly stimulating as more members shed their natural reticence and actively participate.

As well as offering classes, workshops and social events, SACC exists to lend its support on a daily basis to women who might be caught up in problematic family situations, women who are struggling against bureaucracy, women who want to make a new life for themselves, women trying to feed their children and keep a roof over their heads. SACC is a place of comfort and support.

TRISHA MIFFLEN

Single Mother; Antigonish, Nova Scotia

THREE YEARS AGO, because of a violent separation from my husband / myself / my life, I came to Antigonish and settled in / unsettled in to a one bedroom apartment with my four children aged one to six. Over a period of some months I slowly lost the fight for sanity and survival. One evening, as feelings of fear for and of myself were beginning to overcome any sense of control that I had, the phone rang.

A woman I had never met began talking to me about a class she gave on women's issues, which she wanted me to attend. She spoke to me as though I were a normal, worthwhile person. She didn't seem to notice that I was totally shy, with no self-esteem and a feeling of being absolutely helpless. She made me feel that I would add something of value to this class of hers and that she really wanted and expected me to go to it.

For days I hung on to the memory of this phone call. I can't remember any definite, immediate event that made me attend that first class. (I hadn't stepped outside the door in weeks.) But I did go, and after that there was no looking back. Through my involvement with this class and through our dreams and work of creating our Women's Association in Antigonish, I stepped out of my former shy, insecure self.

Today I receive a large part of my feelings of satisfaction, joy and love from the support work I do with other women who are experiencing what I went through. To pass on to each the knowledge that she is not alone and that she has the right to feel as she does is wonderful. There's no greater feeling of pride and happiness, knowing that she, too, will come out on top and survive.

THE MONTREAL ASSAULT PREVENTION CENTRE

Lisa Weintraub and Leona Heillig; Montreal, Quebec

IN OUR APPROACH to the prevention of violence, instead of giving rules (don't talk to strangers, don't go out at night alone, don't wear a miniskirt), we help develop psychological and physical tools of awareness and response. As vulnerable people, we need to learn how to take care of ourselves so we can make choices in our lives. This empowering, feminist approach to assault prevention is the philosophy underlying all the work we do at the Montreal Assault Prevention Centre, whether working with children, adolescents, parents, school personnel, women or the general public.

We believe that our socialization is at the root of our vulnerability. Everyone has certain rights, and the instinctual sense that these rights are not being respected is our most reliable guide to self-protection. Knowing self-defense techniques is only useful to one who believes she has the right to be safe and make choices.

We start with the very young and work on the premise that a strong sense of self-worth is essential to a person's safety and well-being. This is also our assumption when working with adolescent boys to help them act in less aggressive ways. A person with high self-esteem will not need to control others in order to feel powerful.

Part of our work is to offer positive, alternative role models to children and teenagers. Our diverse teams of animators are made up of assertive, gentle women and men. They respect what people say and talk about respecting other people's choices as well as protecting our right to make our own.

By challenging mainstream views of leadership, peer relations and education, we hope to change our own and others' relationship to power and strength.

NORTHERN LIGHTS RESOURCE ASSOCIATION AND CRISIS LINE

Hannah Murphy, Theresa Whitson, Bea Kine; Westlock, Alberta

WHEN NORTHERN LIGHTS Resource Association and Crisis Line became incorporated as a nonprofit organization, we went to our municipalities to ask for a per capita grant to set up a safe place for women experiencing family violence. In one breath our municipal fathers said "no" while in the next breath one man told of a woman being chased across the field by her husband who was carrying a shotgun — "Right in my division; she sure could run." *We* were not laughing.

We get referrals from doctors, the RCMP, social services, ministers and teachers, but we still hear people say that we don't have a problem in "our community." We get calls of all kinds — runaway kids, unwed mothers, suicide calls and abused women and kids. We've had several women with forty-five or fifty years of "wedded bliss" finally come to us with bruises all over their bodies. Some did leave and have found new lives for themselves; some haven't.

On talking with abused women we realized they didn't want to go to a big city shelter. It was traumatic enough having to leave their homes and everything they'd helped to build over the years. We've tried to get a shelter in our area under Project Haven, through Canada Mortgage and Housing, but to no avail. And so we will have another raffle this fall to raise funds to help transport these "nonexistent" battered and beaten women.

LOUKY BERSIANIK

Writer; Verchères, Quebec

WE MUST ALL RECOGNIZE, at last, that misogyny is cultural and institutional, and that it acts insidiously on the brain and behaviour of every man and woman on this planet. Patriarchal cultures are ALL violent towards women, a violence not isolated, not accidental and not the work of madness but a systematic, daily violence, both physical and mental.

Down through the centuries, in all ages and in every social climate, humanity has taken part in this bloody quadrille which divides human beings into two categories – the men on one side, the women on the other – to identify clearly those whom one can crush, massacre, mutilate, beat to death and annihilate with impunity.

"In male fantasy," says Robbe-Grillet, "woman's body is the privileged place of violation." Only in fantasy, says this sanctimonious fellow! Fantasies like the selective butchery at the Polytechnique, like the odious injunction on the body of Chantal Daigle, like the gang rape at McGill? Fantasies like the women who are beaten daily or murdered by the men in their lives, who are raped, tortured, burned alive for the lack of a dowry, who are sold or prostituted? Fantasies like the little girls subjected to incest, pornography, clitoridectomies, infibulation, dismemberment, murder? Fantasies like the innumerable news items worthy of the pages of *Allô Police*? "Don't touch our fantasies," bawl the Robbe-Grillets of free expression, "They don't hurt anyone!!" ENOUGH IS ENOUGH!

Il faut que tous les êtres humains comprennent enfin que la misogynie est culturelle et institutionnelle, et qu'elle agit insidieusement sur la matière grise et le comportement de chaque homme et de chaque femme de cette planète. TOUTES les cultures patriarcales sont violentes envers les femmes, d'une violence non pas isolée, non pas accidentelle, ni le fait de quelque cerveau atteint de folie, mais d'une violence systématique et quotidienne, tant psychologique que physique.

Depuis des centaines de siècles, à toutes les époques et dans n'importe quel climat social, on assiste à ce quadrille sanglant qui sépare les êtres humains en deux catégories: les hommes d'un côté, les femmes de l'autre, pour bien identifier ceux qu'on pourra écraser, massacrer, mutiler, battre à mort, réduire à néant, en toute impunité.

"Dans les fantasmes masculins, dit Robbe-Grillet, le corps de la femme est le lieu privilégié de l'attentat." Seulement dans les fantasmes, nous dit ce bon apôtre! Fantasmes que cette tuerie sélective à Polytechnique, que cette odieuse injonction sur le corps de Chantal Daigle, que ce viol collectif à McGill? Fantasmes que ces femmes battues tous les jours, que ces femmes assassinées par l'homme de leur vie, que ces femmes violées, torturées, brûlées vives à défaut de dot, que ces femmes vendues, prosti-tuées? Fantasmes que ces petites filles inces-tuées, pornographiées, clitoridectomisées, infibulées, dépecées, assassinées? Fantasmes que ces innombrables faits divers dignes d'Allô Police? "Ne touchez pas à nos fantasmes," braillent les Robbe-Grillet de la libre expression. "Ils ne font de mal à personne!!" TROP C'EST TROP!

KATE BRAID

Carpenter, Poet
Vancouver, British Columbia

All right you guys, you win!
Here's one more
hell of a hot day and you all
have bare chests and
once too often you've asked
that stunningly witty question
When will you *take off* your *T-shirt, Kate?*

So here I go! Open your eyes and look!
No T-shirt now, just me
and my skin feels great
in the cool tingle of breeze
at last drying sweat.
Already I feel brown all over.
Why haven't I done this
                    sooner?

What?
It embarrasses you to see
my biceps flash
when I swing this hammer?
You never knew it was muscle
            beneath all those curves?

You want what?
No brother. When the shirt comes off
it's off.
You'll simply have
to lower your eyes
when the woman walks by.

JUDY MARCHAND

Activist, Potter; Brandon, Manitoba

MY MOTHER WAS A STRONG WOMAN. She had twelve children. When we lived in towns where there was no running water or electricity, she heated water from the pump and washed clothes by hand. Usually there was a baby. When she was trying to remember the date of an event, she would say, "Now who was the baby then?" One year four of us had measles at the same time. We stayed in bed in a darkened room. Every now and then, Mom would come in with water, soup and cool hands.

Her hands were always busy. In the fall, the house was filled with smells of spices and simmering fruit as she made up a winter's supply of pickles, relish and jams. In September, she would begin knitting our tuques, mittens and scarves for the winter.

Sometimes she would lose her patience and yell at us, but it would blow over. I don't remember her spanking us. She read the newspaper closely and listened to the radio. She could get really worked up about political events.

When I became active in the women's movement, there were many issues on which my mother and I did not agree. Yet my sense of what was possible had been formed by seeing her do what she had to do. My mother's commitment had been to keep her family going in the face of poverty and isolation; my commitment was to be part of changing the way women could live their lives.

Recently, my mother's busy hands and active mind have been quieted by several small strokes. At eighty-three, she has become childlike. I go to her hospital room and brush her hair, help her to walk, get her ready for bed and reassure her that she is loved and will be cared for. At times, I feel I am my mother's mother.

MARIAN YEO

Activist, Art Critic; Winnipeg, Manitoba

IN 1975 THE WINNIPEG ART GALLERY announced that the theme of its exhibition in honour of International Women's Year would be the *image* of women in art. Because almost all the recognized artists at the time were male, women would be presented as passive models rather than active artists. I joined a group of women artists to protest the show.

We saw discrimination against women in the art system as twofold. First, women had not been recognized as serious professionals and up to that time few were accepted as part of the canon. Second, women's life experiences are not identical to men's, and the exciting part of feminist art was the new images that reflected unique female experiences. We felt that this was the type of work that rightfully should be displayed for International Women's Year.

Our persistence paid off when the gallery director agreed to our request for space to mount a feminist counter-show. In just a few months we organized the exhibition and raised the money to pay for it.

Our counter-exhibition, "Woman As Viewer," included works by women from every province in Canada as well as by a few US artists. Our goal was to show that women working in all modes of art production were as talented and skilled as male artists. The exhibition was a smashing success and received more publicity than any art exhibition in Winnipeg before or since. Our galleries were crowded throughout the show, and people who had never been to an art gallery came to see works of art that had relevance to their own lives.

JILLIAN RIDINGTON

Former Chairperson, The BC Periodical Review Board
Vancouver, British Columbia

I BEGAN TO SEE PORNOGRAPHY AS a form of violence against women when I worked at the Vancouver Transition House during the mid-seventies. I met many women there who had been forced into acts inspired by pornography. I heard of their attempts to divert their mates or to appease the men's anger at their refusal. Inevitably the attempts were unsuccessful — they gave in, were beaten or both. Their mates' behaviour seemed to emanate from minds which did not experience the world in the same way as did the victims. I began to see pornography as a means by which a frightening mentality was shaped and to feel that feminism would not be able to deal with any of the forms that sexual violence took unless feminists understood pornography.

Whereas erotica is about sex that empowers both partners, pornography is about sex as an expression of power over another human being. In its language and its images pornography is anti-human and anti-sex. It inhibits human understanding and limits true communication.

Pornography not only depicts violence against women, children and some men; it also is violence and a legitimation of violence. Pornography preys on the fears of men who are afraid of women or of intimacy. It exploits the frustration we all experience with the difficulties of conducting intimate relationships. But it has no answers for the problems of real life. Rather, it inhibits the communications that might bring about their resolution.

Good sex education that emphasizes intimacy, sensitivity and joy is our most effective antidote to pornography, since most people do not link sex with domination unless taught to do so.

MUMS

Mothers United for Metro Shelter; Halifax, Nova Scotia

WE ARE A GROUP OF low-income, single parents, mainly residents and ex-residents of Bryony House, a safe house for battered women and children. Driven by concern for the situation facing homeless women and children in transition houses, we joined together to protest the lack of affordable housing in the Halifax/Dartmouth area. With housing availability at less than one half percent, landlords can pick and choose their tenants. Single parents on social assistance are usually the last on the list.

We provide a unified voice to bring the lack of affordable housing to the attention of the provincial government and the public. We have written letters and explained our situation to various government officials. We've staged protest marches. We served a symbolic eviction notice on the officials of Province House. We have worked with other housing lobby groups, spoken out at committee hearings and pleaded our case every way we could.

MUMS also serves as a haven, a shelter for its own members. At our meetings we share our personal joys and troubles in an atmosphere of understanding and acceptance. We also encourage the public to contact us. Since many of us have gone through crisis situations of our own, we can offer firsthand knowledge and support in many different areas. It has been recognized that where you see the MUMS you will see confidence, strength, determination, loyalty and a desire to help. We open our arms to anyone who wishes to join or support us and, more important, to anyone in need of our support.

ELIZABETH CUSACK WALSH

Lawyer; Sydney, Nova Scotia

VIVID MEMORIES OF the inhumanity in our courts — I remember a judge saying that a husband who attacked his terrified wife with two serrated knives couldn't have meant any harm. I have waited months and years for important custody cases or maintenance matters to be heard because insurance, business or criminal cases have taken priority. I have seen husbands get probation for crimes against their families for which ordinary citizens would get severe jail sentences.

Women lawyers are often exposed publicly to sexist insults in courtrooms, but I have some memories few will be ambitious to match. In 1978 I defended a young man on a serious criminal charge. His preliminary inquiry was three and one half weeks after the birth of my daughter, and I was anxious to ensure that her nursing schedule wouldn't be interrupted. Although noon hour adjournments are normally long enough for a very relaxed meal, the judge refused to grant me enough time to go home to nurse my daughter. He thought my request frivolous.

By mid-afternoon I was in deep distress, mentally and physically. Milk began spurting through my clothes, all over my cross-examination notes. The courtroom was crowded with spectators. I was standing, cross-examining an RCMP scientist on a very technical point. The judge was enraged when I requested a few minutes adjournment. When he cooled down, I explained that I was leaking milk, that my notes were wet and that I would like a few minutes to deal with the situation. The judge remembers the incident as a joke. I remember how women and motherhood were degraded.

Clearly, we have a long way to go before we can say that in concrete terms there is true equality before the law in Canada.

NELLIE'S HOSTEL FOR WOMEN

Toronto, Ontario

ONE WEARS MANY HATS as a member of the Nellie's Collective — counsellor, cook, financial administrator, charwoman, fundraiser, maintenance woman and policy developer — to name a few. We share all duties. The most menial tasks may be decided by the flip of a coin. Most everything else to do with running the hostel is determined collectively at our weekly meetings. These are also the times when we share the tribulations and joys of life at Nellie's.

Nellie's is a shelter for homeless women and children. It is quite different from a battered women's shelter, though most of our residents have been abused at some point in their lives. The youngest resident we ever had was three hours old; the oldest was in her nineties. They arrive from a variety of backgrounds and countries. They leave behind violent mates, alcoholic parents, rooming houses with scarey neighbours, situations where they have been sexually assaulted, gloomy jail cells, drug and alcohol rehabilitation centres, terrifying psychiatric wards and even dingy stairwells or lonely, breezy parks. They come seeking food and shelter and a sympathetic ear.

Although minor skirmishes can occur over channel selection in the TV room or noisy nocturnal wanderings, the common bond of homelessness and the sharing of stories in a non-punitive atmosphere generally keeps things congenial. The bonds that women form at Nellie's can last for many years. Each Sunday we hold a big dinner, inviting all former residents as well as one member of the board of directors. We sort through donated clothing, and everyone helps out in the kitchen. Many women keep in touch through this program; thus the Nellie's community grows each year. And so, amid the sounds of despair and laughter, the blaring of radios and the babbling of babies, Nellie's moves on into its second decade.

SHIRLEY BEAR

Artist, Activist; Tobique, New Brunswick

THE CREATOR, TO ME, means more than just a personage that is to be praised or prayed to. It is not just male or female but a wonderful combination of the two — and beyond. I do not feel that I stand apart from the greater intelligence of this Creation but that I participate in the activity of it.

Equality is a concept open to interpretation. People can sometimes manipulate the meaning of equality to suit their narrow ideas. Creation gives rights of equality to all the creatures.

When I gather plants or roots, I never deplete an area of its gifts. Rather, some has to be left in order to promote future harvests. And a thanksgiving must always be given in order to assure the Creator that I understand the value of the gifts.

Look at a man and understand the wants and needs and value of this person; look at a woman and understand the wants and needs and value of this person; look at a child and understand the wants and needs and value of this person; and respect each, no matter what your personal opinion might be.

With all the respect for persons and nature that I feel, I also understand the process of survival in our Creation. The baby seals issue was never what it is until greed went hunting. The air was never hard to breathe until greed went digging. And greed became god.

URSULA FRANKLIN

Professor of Metallurgy and Materials Science; Toronto, Ontario

WHEN, AS A CHILD, my interests turned to science, I dreamt of entering a world of respect for knowledge. There would be, I thought, reverence for the beauty and logic of nature's laws. There would be no bias, only the unassailable quest for truth. How wrong I was.

The laws of nature have no bias, but those who interpret them do. It took me a while to understand that the notions of value-free knowledge and neutral technologies were nothing but fortifications for the defence of the status quo. Whether hierarchal structures are intellectual or social and political, modern science and technology serve these structures and perpetuate them.

It was my intense involvement in the peace movement and the women's movement, largely through the group Voice of Women, that provided me with a different perspective for my professional work. To what purpose is knowledge accumulated? For whose benefit is the new information being used? So began my preoccupation with the structure of modern technology and its impact on the world in which we live. More and more I worked on the social meaning of technology, both ancient and modern. This is an area that engages my heart and my mind.

In our common search for a way to change the violent and destructive world around us, I continue to rely on the spread of feminist and pacifist practices as my source of optimism and hope.

JUDY DAVIS AND JUNE DALEY

Environmentalists; Tatamagouche, Nova Scotia

WE WERE BOTH BORN AND RAISED in the coal-mining town of Westville, Nova Scotia, the children of working-class and welfare families. We have been living together for twelve years now. We share the dream of a better life for all on this planet. The dream is expressed by our life-style and by our involvement in local and international issues.

Since we were in our teens we have been involved in struggles to improve many conditions in our home community, doing advocacy work on legal, housing and welfare issues. Judy writes songs and poems which portray reality as she has viewed it from "the other side of the tracks." Presently our main activities are in the peace and environmental movements, which we see as one.

We believe that social change will take place in society only when each of us takes control of her life by refusing work that contributes to the destruction of the earth and by refusing to be seduced into living the modern life-style, which we feel is destructive spiritually and environmentally.

We left school early and do not regret having done so, since we are both independent and feel that the lack of a public education has contributed to that independence.

For the last six years we have lived near Tatamagouche, about forty miles from our home town of Westville. We live in a small log house which we built ourselves. We also built a log barn which is shared by our dog, our cat, a beautiful quarter horse mare and our chickens. We are striving to be as self-sufficient as possible in today's world.

54

THE PICTOU COUNTY
WOMEN'S CENTRE

New Glasgow, Nova Scotia

THE WOMEN'S CENTRE IS our feminist home, a source of support and comfort, a place to work as activists. Because we live in a small, rural community, we don't have a big choice in feminist groups; we can't specialize in our activism. This makes our group quite diverse. Also, our work at the centre puts us in touch with many women who would not identify themselves as feminists but who discover that our struggles are the same as theirs.

Since 1974 we have been working with and without money, wanting funding but not wanting to become institutionalized, trying to maintain our focus despite the pressures of other political agendas. Sometimes it seems as though we are constantly struggling to define ourselves and to fight off the forces which work to keep us down.

We strive to be a strong and united group, finely tuned to our collective needs. We challenge ourselves and what we have been taught, searching for alternatives to patriarchal hierarchy. Working here is more than a job; rarely does the work stay behind when we go home. Many of us are friends, as well, and share other parts of our lives. We try to hold each other together in tough times.

We are feminist, socialist, heterosexual, lesbian, celibate. We have children; we have no children. We live in town; we live in the country. We are from Pictou County; we are from away. We struggle together to work collectively, committed to sharing information and knowledge about women with women and in so doing to make changes in the world.

56

LINDA CHRISTIANSEN-RUFFMAN

Sociologist, Former President of CRIAW
Ferguson's Cove, Nova Scotia

In graduate school I was trained by famous men and in the scholarly traditions of famous men. Though successful, the more I learned the more I became disturbed by the pervasive elitism, individualism and sexism of this realm. My informal education blossomed when I went to work in Nova Scotia and Labrador where the wisdom of "ordinary women" revealed the limits of professional expertise and practice. My discovery that sociological theories did not work in these communities kindled my search for new, feminist ways of working and knowing.

Doing feminist research means collaborating. The kitchen table with all its female symbolism and pragmatism is often the site for such research — collecting information, analyzing experiences, planning videos, organizing conferences, writing briefs. Typically, a meeting takes place at the home of the least mobile member, with kids wandering through and daily life grounding the abstractions.

Work that began independently around such kitchen tables in Ottawa and Halifax grew into CRIAW, the Canadian Research Institute for the Advancement of Women, with publications, annual conferences, research projects and data-banks. CRIAW insists that all kinds of women can take part in research and that the results legitimately take many forms. I like to think of CRIAW as "a research institute without walls" — helping women across the country to participate jointly and to share information.

While differing greatly around Canada and the world, feminist research shares the common objective of collecting information useful for social change. As we discover together the different manifestations of patriarchal oppression, we become better equipped to transform the world.

MARGRIT EICHLER

Sociologist; Toronto, Ontario

IF WE LOOK AT PRESENT GLOBAL PROBLEMS, I would list three: the danger of annihilating life on earth through total warfare (atomic, biological or chemical), the gradual destruction of the natural environment and the new reproductive technologies (NRTs). Most people would see the third (NRTs) as a blessing. Why, then, do I see them as such an enormous threat?

Some of the clients now seeking NRTs are doing so because they have been damaged by previous medical interventions — DES, the Dalkon Shield, etc. Others experience infertility caused by environmental conditions or preventable social problems such as malnutrition, untreated sexually transmitted diseases, and so forth. Inventing ways to circumvent the resulting problems helps to hide the root causes. If we can freeze semen and ova, why clean up a work place that is hazardous to the reproductive systems of the workers?

NRTs lead inevitably to the industrialization of human reproduction and thus to the loss of that which makes us human. The new prenatal diagnostic techniques have turned pregnancy into a time of anxiety in which fetuses are subjected to quality control and women are forced to make eugenic decisions. Behind the rapid development of NRTs is a billion dollar industry looking to make profits from the human body and human reproduction. NRTs have been developed not because we know so much about how our reproductive systems function but because we know so little. We have already seriously endangered the ecological balance of this planet with our cumulative interventions. Now we are starting to do the same with the human body. After that, what will be left?

DIANE DUGGAN

Rape Crisis Worker; St. John's, Newfoundland

I SEE RAPE AS REPRESENTING the reality of women's lives. It is at the end of a continuum which includes all levels of our oppression. The fear of rape constantly reminds all women of our second-class status. That fear has been the most useful tool that men have created to keep us "in line." So, even though all men don't rape, all men benefit from its reality.

We once believed, naively, that awareness was the key and that once men realized how many women and children were being abused, steps would be taken to correct the problem. In developing an analysis of why our oppression was continuing and even escalating, it became clear that the male-controlled systems which regulate our society had no interest in changing anything! Government, organized religion, the legal system, medicine, education, the media and the economy all feed and flourish on women's oppression.

We know now that we are taking part in a revolution that will drastically change the world. We will settle for nothing less than a society which truly values women and children. For this reason, I have no choice but to be a radical feminist. No woman does. I want what all women want: a world with limitless possibilities, where caring and dignity are the norm, where there is no fear for our children and our land — a world where violence is a forgotten word.

THE CANADIAN ABORTION RIGHTS ACTION LEAGUE (CARAL)

Toronto, Ontario

"WHEN I WAS YOUNG, a woman I knew had an illegal abortion. I was there when she began to hemorrhage. Someone called an ambulance. As people helped her into the ambulance, she died."

"I put a teenage member of my family on a bus to get an abortion in New York before the law was changed in Canada. The family didn't know. I can't remember today how we scraped the money together. How sad that was, sending her to New York, alone."

"A friend had to have an illegal abortion when she was in her late teens. She is married now and has two daughters, but her memories of that lonely time are still strong. Neither she nor I ever want her daughters to suffer as she did."

"I got pregnant at seventeen and phoned doctors, looking for an abortion. One referred me to the Catholic Children's Aid! Then I answered a "Pregnant and Distressed" ad in the newspaper; I didn't know it was an anti-choice group. They called regularly, telling me I would be a murderer and threatening to tell my parents."

"One March my mother took me to hear Dr. Henry Morgenthaler speak. That December I had had an ectopic pregnancy almost immediately after the insertion of an IUD. It had taken doctors three months to figure it out, while I was in excruciating pain and could have died. At that meeting, everything clicked."

Our stories differ in one respect: sometimes the experience with an unwanted pregnancy happened to us and sometimes to another woman. But it is typical of the empathy women feel for one another that we reacted in the same way — by becoming involved with this issue, which is a touchstone of feminism.

MONIQUE DAUPHIN

Assault Prevention Teacher; Montreal, Quebec

I'M FORTY-TWO YEARS OLD. I immigrated to Canada from Haiti in 1969. As a black woman, a mother, a worker, a student, one who is poor and a feminist, I've had to rise to many challenges. First I've had to integrate myself, a black woman, into my adopted society, which is patriarchal and white. As well, I've had to provide for family who stayed behind and later help them immigrate. A single mother of three, I foster my children's Haitian identity here in Canada.

I work part time at the Montreal Assault Prevention Centre. This experience allows me to explore deeply the curse of violence against women and children and to get a better understanding of how to deal with it. That is also my academic field of study, which I have had to abandon twice without finishing my degree for the sake of my duties as a mother. This, too, prolongs my economic insecurity, my poverty.

I reject all sexist stereotyping and teach my children to think for themselves and challenge obsolete ideas. My daughters already have a degree of consciousness, but what about the others? What about my son? Our sons?

This is my great challenge and that of all women who struggle to change social behaviour and improve male-female relations. Have we lived up to this challenge? As for me, I affirm that thanks to my feminist approach, thanks to the support of other women and in spite of my great difficulties, I am strong, happy, and I continue to struggle.

J'ai quarante-deux ans. Je suis d'origine haïtienne, immigrée au Canada depuis 1969. Femme noire, mère, travailleuse, étudiante, féministe et pauvre, j'ai dû relever des défis! D'abord, en tant que femme noire, je devais m'intégrer à ma société d'adoption, patriarcale et blanche. Ensuite, j'ai dû pourvoir aux besoins de ma famille restée au pays et plus tard la faire immigrer. En tant que mère monoparentale de trois enfants, je leur inculque l'identité haïtienne au Canada.

Je travaille à temps partiel au Centre de prévention des agressions de Montréal. Cette expérience me permet d'approfondir le fléau de la violence faite aux femmes et aux enfants, et de mieux saisir l'intervention psychosociologique. Celà est aussi mon champ d'études, que j'ai dû abandonner à deux reprises sans terminer mon baccalauréat au profit de mes fonctions de mère. Ce qui, entre autres, perdure mon insécurité économique, ma pauvreté.

Je refuse tout stéréotype sexiste et inculque à mes enfants un esprit critique face à certaines valeurs rétrogrades. Mes filles sont déjà assez averties, mais qu'en est-il des autres? Qu'en est-il de mon fils? De nos fils?

C'est mon grand défi, et celui de toutes les femmes qui militent pour changer les comportements et améliorer les rapports hommes-femmes. Avons-nous relevé ce défi? Et moi, j'affirme que grâce à mon cheminement féministe, grâce au soutien des femmes, et malgré mes grandes difficultés, je suis forte, heureuse et je continue à me battre.

66

LYNNE FERNIE

Artist, Filmmaker, Editor; Toronto, Ontario.

I REMEMBER THE DISTINCT MOMENT when I realized that I'd been had. It was four a.m. on a Sunday morning in 1976, and I'd stayed up all night reading *The Female Eunuch*. That was the night I realized that I'd been taught to interpret my life through systematically instituted prejudices which are invisibly embedded in our culture.

Since then, my analyses have changed and expanded as our theories and strategies for ways to affect our culture have progressed. Feminism has provided the ground for me — a white woman — to begin to understand systemic oppression in terms of race and class. It has provided me as an individual woman with the theoretical and actual community in which to make choices outside the bounds of social prescription.

Many feminist women, like myself, live personal lives nourished sexually as well as emotionally and intellectually by other women. That this lesbian aspect of our history may be marginalized by being absent or not fully present even within our self-representations is evidence that we have not yet constructed a sufficiently safe political or moral territory in which to speak.

ESTHER SHANNON

Journalist, Former Editor of Kinesis
Vancouver, British Columbia

THE MAINSTREAM MEDIA has a lot of rules about objectivity and balance and keeping a reporter out of a story. These rules assume that commitment to a point of view means the truth will not be told. They assume that there is a truth, something you get to see daily on the front page for fifty cents.

But until feminism, women rarely saw any truths about themselves on the front pages. Until feminism, the dailies' front page truths managed to coexist with the virtual silencing of fifty percent of the globe, and no one even noticed.

In the early seventies, feminists founded newspapers to give women a voice. Feminist newspapers didn't believe in objectivity; they didn't advocate balanced reporting. Most of them didn't even have any reporters. They did, however, have an incredible number of true stories.

Many of the most profound social and economic issues discussed today were first reported in the feminist press. Examples, unhappily, abound: rape, wife battering, sexual harassment, child sexual abuse, incest. Critical economic issues such as the wage gap, employment ghettos, the feminization of poverty and the double workload were all first exposed by the feminist press.

Perhaps more significant than any one piece of coverage was the fact that these stories arose, and still arise, from the women who experienced them. Usually there is no reporter in the story; there are participants. And with these participants we build an analysis of women's lives that constantly expands feminism.

PAT LESLIE

The Women's Movement Archives; Toronto, Ontario

THE WOMEN'S MOVEMENT ARCHIVES is an independent collection documenting the grass-roots organizing of the women's liberation movement. The earliest material was culled from a haphazard collection of files belonging to *The Other Woman*, a Toronto feminist newspaper of the mid-seventies. During the first five years that I collected material, the archives lived with me in my home. In the early eighties I found other interested women, and we formed a collective which later became a nonprofit organization.

In building the feminist archives, we focused on two goals. First, we had to find women who would catalogue the collected material and make it accessible to other women. In this process, we acknowledged regional autonomy, agreeing that material produced in any given area should stay there, kept in a safe and accessible location.

Second, and in some ways more important, we wanted to build consciousness among women that history is not merely something that happened a long time ago. What we are living becomes history. We censor ourselves by not writing down our thoughts, by not keeping what we have written, by throwing away leaflets publicizing demonstrations, or by overlooking even the importance of keeping minutes at group meetings.

Change is effected through the efforts of many people working together. None of the groups whose papers or publications are kept in the archives can be fully understood without recognition of the great impact made on them by all of their members. The archives project is about putting women back into history, through our own eyes and in our own way.

BETTY BAXTER

Athelete; Vancouver, British Columbia

I BECAME A FEMINIST after being fired as coach of Canada's National Women's Volleyball Team in 1982. The firing was based on rumours about my sexual orientation and resulted in my coming out publicly as a lesbian in sport. It wasn't just anger and hurt at being fired that directed me to feminism but also my need to understand those mysterious injustices that kept women out of positions, like my former job, where they could effect change.

I was and am determined to create a place where women and young girls can experience sport in a positive way, learning about their physical, psychological and emotional strengths. At my volleyball club in Vancouver any girl or woman is welcome. There are highly skilled players and novices. My vision is to have enough variety in the membership that everyone can be someone else's model.

Do feminism and competitive sport mix? I think they do. The needs of the group come first, but as a coach I'm working with all the players to help them grow, trust each other and reach their full potential as volleyball players and as people, too. A goal might be that we finish each year kinder to ourselves, charitable to our opponents and still having the desire to improve. Thus we work on our strengths, coming to realize how skilled and strong we really are. Winning and losing games are just steps along the way to that realization. This belief in the skills and strengths of women is a cornerstone of my feminism.

KRIS PURDY AND HEATHER BISHOP
Musicians, Singer-songwriters; Winnipeg, Manitoba

MUSIC, A LIFE'S PASSION, a voice for energy, the energy of women rising and expanding, taking to ourselves the power that has always been there.

Music, the mucilage that has bound the two of us together since those first days. It was 1971, and we had just escaped Toronto. The Abortion Caravan had marched to Ottawa the year before; the Vietnam war was still unresolved; the idea of Quebec independence was burning itself into the Canadian consciousness, and Women's Studies was a new discipline. And here we were, feasting on the sensuousness of vigorous winds, the wonder of deceptively fragile flowers, the magic of sky cradling it all. We were on the prairie, where time and space released energy and the silence carried harmony. Suddenly music was in our lives, ready to lead us down myriad paths.

Music, the magnet that in 1973 pulled together a motley crew for Saskatchewan's first women's dance band — Walpurgis Night — playing all those familiar tunes, familiar yet different. The notes were the same; the words were the same, yet different, coming from a woman.

Music, that tough mistress, a craft to learn and respect, demanding study and practice, forcing a connection with the "business" of tours, albums, producers, promoters where we flourish and flounder, and still the music remains. Music, those notes and words that keep filling us with everything that's bigger than ourselves. Okay, then, let's go — singing and dancing — till we drop!

THE BIRTH CONTROL AND VD INFORMATION CENTRE

Toronto, Ontario

FOR TOO LONG information concerning women's health has been within reach of medical personnel alone. The Birth Control and VD Information Centre offers a nontraditional health service. We provide women with knowledge about their bodies and especially their reproductive systems and try to counter the typical power dynamic between a woman and her physician. We come from varying educational backgrounds. In this work it's not formal training that's important but rather a way of listening and empathizing, respectfully laying out the choices and letting the woman decide what she wants.

Half of our work is done at the clinic; the rest is community programing. At the clinic we counsel women about birth control, sexually transmitted diseases, pregnancy and abortion. We act as an advocate for the patient when she meets the doctor to be sure that her needs and concerns are heard. Young women may be more knowledgeable about their bodies than they were twenty years ago, but many still lack assertiveness skills. By putting them in control in the doctor's office we help them through potentially scarey or embarrassing situations such as a first pelvic exam, a diaphragm fitting or treatment for an infection.

In our community program, we go to schools, prisons, psychiatric centres, hostels — wherever we're asked. Usually the topic is contraception, but we'll tackle almost any women's health issue: menopause, sexual assault, puberty. Getting out of the clinic and into the community keeps us in touch with what's on people's minds.

THE CRONEYS

Women's Support Group; Winnipeg, Manitoba

WOMEN'S SUPPORT GROUPS abounded during the seventies and eighties. Each woman belonged for her own particular reason, and each group functioned in its unique way. But taken together, these support groups were the foundation upon which the modern-day women's movement was built.

When we began meeting in 1983, we named ourselves The Croneys to claim the reference to aging women and to separate ourselves from the idea of a group of male companions or cronies. Our journey together has always been varied, rarely been smooth. Expectations ran high, and we have not always succeeded in meeting them. From the beginning, no matter how large or small the group, we struggled with questions of process, structure and content.

But, despite the pain of trying to meet everyone's needs, each of us has grown tremendously through our group experience. Those of us with children found that sharing that part of our lives enriched our parenting skills. We took wilderness canoe trips together and found individual and collective strength we had never imagined we had. We discussed the real issues in our lives and grew to understand that our powerlessness is rooted in a patriarchal society that flourishes by subjugating women. We explored and embraced feminist ideals that will remain with us the rest of our lives.

SHELLEY FINSON

United Church Minister, Educator; Toronto, Ontario

VERY OFTEN I am asked, "How can you be a feminist and a Christian?" and I reply, "It isn't easy!" For me, a Christian woman ordained and committed to working within the Christian community, there are many basic tensions.

To begin with, my faith has had to be totally re-visioned. Also, the meaning of my ministry has had to shift to include the significance of patriarchy in all our lives. I see myself called to be beside women who are bound by a theology that does not offer freedom or hope but which keeps them enslaved to old images and to dehumanizing roles. And when working with men, there is always the challenge of how to call them to take responsibility for their power and privilege.

Most difficult and at the same time most exciting are the personal shifts that I have had to make as I have come to know myself as woman, as feminist. The difficulty lies in constantly recognizing that the church requires me to live a double life. Rarely is it possible to be authentically myself. I must swallow my responses to what I see, hear and feel.

There are times, when together with other women, that we remember that our faith calls us to work for a world without oppression or privilege. Then we recall our sisters of the past — the Goddess, the woman priest, the female saints and martyrs, the witches and pioneers, our mothers. Being a feminist in the Church makes no sense at all except when I recognize the potential for ministry with women and the place that this particular structure might have in creating a different world.

JANICK BELLEAU

Poet; Winnipeg, Manitoba

I've a head like a Tuscan bouillabaisse.
Everything goes in:
my bookfilled future and sleeping dreams of glory.

> *Suddenly,*
> *your lips, salt sip of Mediterranean,*
> *revive*
> *my life sense,*
> *my essence.*

Then the triumphal voice of Galli-Curci,
                                never heard,
strikes my ear.
> *I am moved by the pure line of your curves.*

Walking into the warm mirror of your simplicity,
I see a cypress battered by the wind.
> *One day,*
> *we will travel to Livourne and Modigliani*
> *will be reborn*
> *under my brush.*
> *... Your reclining body, alluring armpit ...*

J'ai la tête comme une bouillabaisse toscane.
Tout y trempe :
mon livre-avenir et mes rêves de gloire en dormant.

> Soudain,
> tes lèvres à la saveur méditerranéenne
> me ravivent
> les sens,
> l'essence.

Puis, la voix triomphale de Galli-Curci,
jamais entendue,
me trouble l'oreille.
> Je m'émeus de la pureté de tes courbes.

Je me recueille dans le chaud miroir de ta simplicité
et j'y vois un cyprès battu par le vent.
> Un jour,
> nous irons à Livourne et Modigliani renaîtra
> sous mon pinceau.
> ... Ton corps allongé, tes aisselles affriolantes ...

REBECCA PRIEGERT COULTER

Educator; Edmonton, Alberta

ALL MY ADULT LIFE I have been a teacher. I am convinced that it really is possible for education to transform lives and that linking learning and activism must be a key strategy for feminists. When I taught Women's Studies at Athabasca University in northern Alberta, I had the exhilarating experience of teaching and learning with adult students, most of whom were women, and saw most clearly the power that comes from linking education and activism.

I can think of so many examples of this power. It was found in the confidence of a former student appearing on the television news to explain the need for a universally accessible, quality child-care system. It was found in the commitment of a group of rural women who took a course together as part of their planning to establish a shelter for battered women. It was found in the activities of a student whose reading on pornography moved her to organize a successful campaign for the removal of hard-core "adult" magazines from the only grocery store in her small town. It was found, too, in the large numbers of women who shared the readings and ideas they discovered in their courses with mothers, sisters, friends and co-workers. And it was found in the women who reported back with pleasure that they had helped someone to understand herself better or to take a stand at work or to see that it was not her fault that she was beaten. As one student said, "The things I learned are around me every day, and my life will never be the same again."

CINDY MURRAY

Farmer; Erickson, Manitoba

I AM THE SIXTH GENERATION farmer since my ancestors came to the New World from Scotland. This country as we know it was built by the pioneers, half of whom were women, women who took an actual, physical part in breaking the land. But unlike their partners on the farm, they had also the children to raise, the meals to cook, the clothes to make and so forth, in addition to the outside work. These women have not been recognized as an important part of the farm, present or past. The term farmer usually refers to the male on the farm.

So what am I, farming on my own? I am the square peg that someone is always trying to pound into the round hole. The bank classifies me as a farmerette. When I insisted that I was a farmer, the bank manager still went ahead and wrote down farmerette. It sends shivers down my back!

Unfortunately, Canada has a cheap food policy which is slowly strangling a way of life — the family farm. Women are doing their work on the farm and then going to town to a paying job as well. My farm is also threatened; therefore I work part-time in town. The time I spend in town is a frustration as I know I should be on the land. If I were receiving the cost of production and a little bit besides, someone in town could have that job. Will I be farming one year from now? Two? Three? How much longer can I hold up against the outside forces that are squeezing, squeezing?

MADELEINE PARENT

Feminist and Union Organizer
Montreal, Quebec

WHEN I WAS SEVEN, my father told me "Some people are very arrogant; don't let anyone walk on you." I remembered this at convent, when obedience was demanded for its own sake. At McGill University, opposition to our campaign for scholarships for poor students and the church hierarchy's opposition to women's right to vote (legislated in 1940) convinced me that the system was intended to disadvantage women and the poor.

During the war I joined the union drive and settled in for the long term, organizing in the textile mills where women worked fifty to fifty-five hour weeks for low wages and where exploitation of child labour was the rule. In 1946, after four difficult years and a strike of 6,000 cotton-mill workers in Valleyfield and Montreal, we made a strategic breakthrough, winning the eight hour day, the single rate list (abolishing lower rates for women) and seniority rights. Women played a strong role. Sunday mornings they sat in church listening to sermons about "woman's place"; Sunday evenings they went to strikers' rallies; Monday mornings at plant gates they took on police, company goons and strike-breakers.

Half a century later, long-standing injustices against women and the disadvantaged persist in a regime where profits come before people. But today's women are better informed; myths about sin and guilt no longer hold sway. I believe young women of all origins and circumstances will continue the struggle in their own way, building coalitions with their sisters around the world and with men who care. They will overcome.

Quand j'avais sept ans, mon père m'a dit: "Dans la vie, tu rencontreras des gens arrogants; ne te laisse pas avoir." Au couvent, je pensais à mon père quand on exigeait l'obéissance sans raison. A l'Université McGill, une campagne pour des bourses gratuites pour étudiant(e)s pauvres a essuyé un dur refus des autorités, justement au temps où la hiérarchie ecclésiale s'opposait au vote des femmes. J'ai compris que le régime désavantageait les femmes et les pauvres.

Durant la guerre, j'ai fait du syndicalisme. Bientôt, je militais auprès des travailleuses et des enfants exploités dans les moulins de coton où leur semaine de travail était de cinquante à cinquante-cinq heures. En 1946, après quatre années d'organisation fortement contestée par les patrons, il y eut une grève de 6000 employé(e)s à Valleyfield et à Montréal. Le dimanche matin à la messe, les femmes entendaient prêcher contre leur syndicat; le soir, elles allaient à l'assemblée des grévistes et le lundi matin, elles confrontaient les briseurs de grève, les "gorilles" de la compagnie et la police. Les travailleurs découvraient en elles des alliées indispensables. La grève a été gagnée.

Aujourd'hui, les injustices à l'endroit des femmes et des personnes désavantagées persistent dans un régime où la course aux profits prime sur les droits humains. Par ailleurs, beaucoup de femmes sont mieux informées et il est plus difficile de les culpabiliser. J'ai confiance que les jeunes femmes — de toutes conditions et origines — continueront la lutte à leur manière. Elles bâtiront des solidarités avec d'autres femmes ici et ailleurs ainsi qu'avec des hommes qui auront compris. Elles réussiront.

SKY BLUE MARY MORIN

Native Activist, Spiritual Teacher
Saskatoon, Saskatchewan

As You lie sleeping
in the winter season
I marvel at your Beauty.
Such a short time to rest
preparing for the work ahead,
My Mother, the Earth Mother
from whence Life comes
in the circle of Life.

Our Mother, the Earth Mother
I see and feel your pain
constantly having to Heal
the wounds of profit makers.
I want to expel my insides
as I watch the chemicals
spew forth from Your Body.
The Scourge and Rape continues.

As Thunder comes to awaken
you from much needed slumber
I see your Rebirth, New Growth.
As you become Forceful
carrying Floods to distant places,
providing paths for Hurricanes,
Quaking from your Insides
I am certain you are strong.

But can you last, Earth Mother?
I pray the offerings of Tobacco
I give to you will help.
I pray our Respect grows
for your Sacredness,
and keeps you Strong;
for should you Cease,
so will the People.

SARA DIAMOND

Artist; Vancouver, British Columbia

MY FASCINATION WITH HISTORY is very personal. My mother died when I was ten, leaving me with little memory of her or my childhood. I spent many years reconstructing her part in my identity, struggling to find her fragments. Some semblance of my mother's historical threads, her traces, could be imagined. From these I constructed *The Influences of My Mother*, one of my first videotapes.

So, what of other women? As my mother's history had been missing, so was that of working-class women in Canada. In 1978 I began the Women's Labour History Project, which has collected many oral histories from working-class women, published resources about these women, toured a photo exhibition and produced videotapes on the history of women and work.

What I desire from history is not simply an insertion into the historical record of some facts and people who were invisible; it is a thorough revisioning. We need a history which speaks to the whole range of behaviour and activities through which women have negotiated the world, from auxiliaries that turned into lobbies, to battered women who could not leave but helped their daughters to achieve independence, to women who led strikes and unions.

The older women we speak to, their stories and wisdom, serve as a bulwark against loss. Each piece that we uncover suggests that history is not a simple, fine, connecting line but many things: ever-moving cycles, a solid rock, a tool.

EUNADIE JOHNSON

Crisis Centre Director; Thompson, Manitoba

THOUGH SOME CHANGES have been made, barriers still exist for black people in Canada, especially for a woman like myself who chooses to live in Northern Manitoba. I feel that the barriers which present themselves on a daily basis have to do with ignorance and a lack of knowledge about black people as a whole. I have experienced blatant and not so blatant racist attitudes in this country. My way of dealing with it is to confront. I do not tolerate anyone thinking I am less than they are. There were times when I would spend time trying to educate, but I feel now that those who want to know can find their own education.

Working with the issue of family violence has not especially endeared me to a community which was willing for a long time to deny the existence of such violence. As a black woman I am immediately recognized and labelled. People greet me with words such as "Are you staying out of trouble, Eunadie?"

Although black women as feminists have to be vocal as oppressed women, they are also fearful of speaking out and being rejected by their own communities. Their communities expect them to focus on the oppression of blacks as a whole and not on a separation of the male and female. When black women suffer oppression from the male in their race and speak out, it is difficult for them not to be considered traitors.

The feminist movement has been seen as a movement of and for white women. My feeling as a feminist is not to accept in totality what the movement espouses but, as an independent, thinking person, to listen and be part of discussions while forming my own opinions.

HARRIET AND SHIRLEY SIMAND

Founders of DES Action Canada; Montreal, Quebec.

WHEN I GOT OVER THE SHOCK of finding out that my mother and I had been exposed to diethylstilbestrol (DES), I tried to get information about DES but met with a blank wall. Diethylstilbestrol was the synthetic estrogen given to pregnant women from 1941 to 1971 to prevent miscarriage. It didn't prevent miscarriage. Instead, it affected the unborn children and the unsuspecting mothers, creating unique medical problems ranging from infertility to cancer.

My mother and I received a grant from Health and Welfare Canada and founded DES Action Canada in 1982. Our inital aim was to educate the public and reach the DES-exposed. We are now a nationwide organization with a doctor's referral list, an extensive reference library, a staff trained to respond to the questions of DES daughters, mothers and sons, and a newsletter on DES research and related issues.

There are many occasions in a woman's life when she may be urged to take hormonal drugs. Before making a decision, she should do her homework and weigh the risks. For centuries women have been able to menstruate, conceive, support gestation, give birth, nurse a child and go through menopause without prescription drugs. We need to think carefully before we allow our endocrine systems to be tampered with. Drugs should be the exception, not the rule. Women have to stand up for themselves and for each other and act as a combined front to reclaim stewardship over their minds and bodies.

WENDY WILLIAMS

President, Provincial Council on the Status of Women
St. John's, Newfoundland

IT'S 1971, AND I AM a brand new university graduate. My first real job — a public health nurse in a rural area of Newfoundland. Part of this job includes visiting women who have been discharged from the cottage hospital with their new babies. One of my first patients is a woman who has just returned to her home with her tenth child. She wants to know what to do. "He hasn't had it for ten days now. I don't want any more children."

The "it" is intercourse. What to say? How to help her get what she wants — birth control?

Birth control had only been legalized two years earlier, in 1969. Abstinence is not an option for this woman, given her husband. She is not a good risk for surgery, so a tubal ligation is not an option. Her husband would not consider a vasectomy; besides, none of the three doctors here do them. There is no drugstore, so there are no condoms. No one fits diaphragms or inserts IUD's. She has asked her doctor for the pill, but he would not give it to her as her blood pressure is too high. The doctor told her to stay away from her husband!

This woman is one of the reasons I have been active in the women's movement, especially in the area of contraceptive services. I believe that for women to be equal two basic things are needed: control over our bodies and economic independence.

LESLIE SPILLETT

Labour Activist; Winnipeg, Manitoba

I GREW UP IN Northern Manitoba, the youngest child of a single-parent, Métis woman. The combination of being a single parent, a Métis and a woman is a sure recipe for poverty. My mother was a woman of remarkable strength and dignity, and although her tradition was not to express herself verbally, she taught her children the power of being proud of who we were.

This has served me well throughout my life, both when I was a child and today. I remember being beaten and called a squaw by a group of boys when I was about eight years old. My instincts were to stand up and fight back against the verbal and physical assault. This instinct remains intact.

After a lot of confusion and pain that must accompany the racism and sexism that I have experienced, I have come to like myself and to know my power. Indeed, I have come to know the power of all people who struggle against those forces with vested interests in maintaining the status quo.

For me, feminism is an extension of my long rebellion against all who would define me by their racist and sexist attitudes. This struggle is not only a personal one, simply to overcome these barriers for my own acceptance. The South African Congress of Trade Unions' slogan, "An injury to one is an injury to all," is one which I try to carry with me into my work in the trade union movement, into my community and also into my personal relationships.

NANCY JACKMAN

Feminist Philanthropist, Political Activist; Toronto, Ontario

I'M A FEMINIST BECAUSE of the relationship I saw between my mom and dad. Watching my mother "give in" to her husband and her sons made me very angry. When my dad died and I inherited some of his wealth, I wanted to use that money so that no woman would have to go through the shame and pain my mother experienced.

Over ninety-eight percent of private foundation funding in Canada goes to men and boys and their institutions. Women with money have a special obligation to address this economic imbalance. Traditionally women give to service organizations. But women of great wealth must give their money to organizations that will get at the root causes of discrimination against women; they must put their money to work for systemic change.

To help women gain political power, I support women at the nomination level in all political parties. I co-founded LEAF (Women's Legal Education and Action Fund), an instrument for challenging the legal discrimination against women. To address economic discrimination against women, I co-founded the Canadian Women's Foundation, which makes funds available to groups that are working towards women's economic independence.

What brought me to these activities? Being a woman and realizing how unfair I'd been to myself and to my mom in blaming her were factors. Being a stuttering, obese child who didn't fit in at school motivated me to notice and protect others who were different. The church removing me from the ministry and my successful legal fight to be reinstated, as well as my dad's death and the struggle over family assets made me realize the power of law and the power of "power." No one has ever done women's work for them, and they won't now. We've got to do it for ourselves.

FOUR THE MOMENT

A Capella Singing Group; Halifax, Nova Scotia

We're here, standing at the shoreline,
Made it through some hard times,
Black mother, Black daughter,
Made it through some hard times.

I see reflections of a past staring at me,
Of work hard and women kneeling to pray.
From the dusk to the dawn,
Each day hard, each day long,
Giving me my claim,
I love you woman.

I see the waters of east shores wearing you grey,
of tides white, but never wearing you down.
With your will, by your might
You have kept gifts of old
Giving me my strength,
I love you woman.

From the weakest one to the strongest one
If we can say who's weak and who's strong,
The wisdom you've given, our blending as women,
To conquer that troubled road,
From your heart, by your life
You have said, be we bold,
Giving me my name,
I love you woman.

I'm a woman Black and a woman first
Cause I know what I have to meet.
Fire and thunder, waters of courage
Are the gifts you've given to me.
For the cause that needs assistance,
Against the wrong that needs resistance
We're still standing
We're still standing...

POWER

Prostitutes and Other Women for Equal Rights
Vancouver, British Columbia

POWER IS A GROUP of prostitute and non-prostitute women working for change and for the equal rights of all women. We are celebrating an anniversary this year — ten years of organizing and lobbying for the rights of sex trade workers.

We see prostitution as work. We believe in and fight for the right of all workers to make our own decisions about the kind of work we do and how we do it. The women who make the decision to enter the sex trade demand the same respect as does any other person in any other job. Sex trade workers don't deserve the violence or verbal and emotional abuse they experience. We believe that women who are trying to survive the best way they know how should not be criminalized and punished by getting arrested, spending time in prison, having their children apprehended and being ostracized by the rest of society.

POWER is run on a shoestring, without government funding. We are accountable to the women we serve. We do front line work as well as lobbying. We have travelled to other countries to talk about poverty and prostitution, and we keep in touch globally with other prostitutes' rights organizations. We produced the first bad-trick sheet ever. Since these are now produced in most major cities across the country, we can take credit where it's due.

We believe in choice in all aspects of our lives and in support for those choices. Women need options and alternatives to prostitution, but if a woman still chooses this as her career, she must have that choice respected.

EVE ZAREMBA

Writer, Publisher; Toronto, Ontario

FOR ALMOST TWENTY YEARS I have played the part of one of those proverbial loud, nasty, bra-burning, shit-kicking, radical "Women's Libbers" that everyone is warned against. Of my almost sixty years these have been the best. And there is more to come.

MARY O'BRIEN

Philosopher, Theorist; Toronto, Ontario

I HAVE CHANGED my job often and have changed my citizenship, too. What hasn't changed is my commitment to feminism and to socialism.

I don't think one job should last a lifetime. I was trained as a nurse and a midwife and did health-related work both in Scotland and Canada. After twenty-five years I had a strong feeling that I knew a lot about what went on in bureaucracy and politics, but I didn't know what it *meant*.

Like so many women, I didn't get to university till I was forty. There I started to study theory. Not much of it made sense to this woman's life — no women, no theory of birth, no theory of male supremacy. Against this I placed the sisterhood, the sense of reality and the urgency of feminism.

What I do now is to try to work out useful theory that makes sense of women's experience. It's marvelously exciting, trying with other women to build the feminist theory around which we discover each other, discover our power, discover our responsibility to make history.

MARIE LAING

Member of the Legislative Assembly; Edmonton, Alberta

I WAS BORN AT HOME in a prairie farm house at the end of the Depression. At the age of nineteen I married. We had four carefully planned children. But we did not live happily ever after. The process of divorce was a consciousness-raising experience for me as it is for most women as we face impoverishment for ourselves and our children. I went to university and became a psychologist. My first "political" work was as director of a rape crisis centre, and it was there I came to know myself as a feminist. When I was asked to be a candidate in the 1986 provincial election, I accepted, believing that change ultimately must come through the political process. Nobody, myself included, expected me to win. But I did.

So, with much misgiving and a sense of wonder, I entered the Legislature, declaring myself an academic, a peace activist, a socialist and a feminist. I feel privileged and humble to have been chosen to serve. For me, being in politics means doing full time what many can do only in their spare time — working for justice and social change. My feminist understanding has been clarified in the years I have served. The challenge I face almost daily is to remain true to the principles which brought me here and to question everything to determine motive. Traditional politics is hierarchical and adversarial, but as a feminist my whole being cries out against narrow interests and justice based on competing rights. For our world to survive we must recognize our interconnection so that concern for our children becomes concern for all children. We must transform the political system by transforming how we think about our world.

THE QUEBEC IMMIGRANT WOMEN'S COLLECTIVE

Montreal, Quebec

IMMIGRANT WOMEN make an important contribution to Quebec society and add to its wealth, yet they are disregarded, almost invisible. Isolated, dependent and often exploited, they are absent from the principal spheres of power, be these political, economic, social or in the trade union movement. And yet women constitute close to half of international immigration.

The Quebec Immigrant Women's Collective works relentlessly to better the position of immigrant women — to improve their living conditions, defend their rights and fight against all forms of racism and sexism. We offer professional training in nontraditional trades. Our top demand centers on universal access for immigrant women to language training that is adapted to their specific schedules and needs.

It takes a dynamic person to make it through the radical process of pulling up one's roots and immigrating. And though this process can be particularly hard on women, it constitutes at times a breaking point, a point of departure towards a life where they take more of their destiny into their own hands. But the development of such autonomy is not automatic. It takes place under certain conditions, and getting together with a group of other women is one of those conditions. Hence the importance of an organization such as the Quebec Immigrant Women's Collective.

Les femmes immigrantes apportent une contribution importante et sont source de richesse pour la société québécoise, mais elles demeurent méconnues, presque invisibles. Isolées, dépendantes et souvent exploitées, elles sont absentes des principaux lieux de pouvoir: politique, économique, social, syndical. Et pourtant les femmes constituent près de la moitié de l'immigration internationale.

Le Collectif des femmes immigrantes du Québec travaille avec acharnement à la promotion du statut des femmes immigrantes, et vise à l'amélioration de leurs conditions de vie, à défendre leurs droits, à lutter contre toute forme de racisme et de sexisme. Nous offrons aussi de la formation professionnelle dans des métiers non traditionnels. Notre revendication prioritaire s'articule autour de l'accès universel pour les femmes immigrantes à la formation linguistique adaptée à leurs rythmes et à leurs besoins spécifiques.

Le dynamisme caractérise souvent les personnes qui traversent un processus aussi radical que celui du déracinement et de l'immigration. Et si ce processus peut être particulièrement lourd pour les femmes, il constitue parfois un point de rupture et un point de départ vers une vie où elles prennent davantage leur devenir en main. Mais le développement de cette autonomie ne va pas de soi. Il se fait dans certaines conditions, et le regroupement des femmes constitue une de ces conditions. Ce postulat ne fait que confirmer toute l'importance d'un organisme tel que le Collectif des femmes immigrantes du Québec.

JOAN MEISTER AND
SHIRLEY MASUDA

DAWN CANADA: DisAbled Women's Network Canada
Vancouver, British Columbia

WHEN DAWN CANADA WAS FOUNDED in 1985 it provided the first national opportunity for women with disabilities to connect with one another and to speak out about issues affecting our lives. Developing our own national voice was important since the disability community was not interested in issues specific to women and the women's movement was not accessible to us.

DAWN CANADA works to bring increased awareness of the situation facing women with disabilities to our members, to others with disabilities and to the consumer's and women's movements. Our issues are women's issues, and all women need to realize that our concerns are their concerns. After all, the incidence of disability increases significantly with age.

We want access to the women's movement and to women's services. We want employment equity. Our priorities include issues of sexuality, health, new reproductive technologies, violence and isolation. By and large, women with disabilities are poor, severely under-employed and lack sex education as well as knowledge of basic health services. We are at least twice as likely as our non-disabled sisters to be the victims of abuse, yet almost no transition houses in Canada are accessible to us. Coercive attitudes can compel us to have unwanted abortions or to become sterilized. Our disabilities make us easy targets for eugenic reproductive technologies, especially in institutionalized settings.

A great deal of work remains to be done. But as we work more closely with our non-disabled sisters and increase our mutual understanding of all we hold in common, our job becomes easier.

MAKING THE CONNECTIONS

Brackley Beach, Prince Edward Island

WE CAME TOGETHER to plan a gathering of women called Making the Connections. We wanted to explore the connections between the status of women, violence against women and global violence. We wanted to examine how these issues are played out in the family, the media and the community and to consider what actions we could take to create a safer world.

Our vision was that Making the Connections should be experiential and holistic. We would have affinity groups and web charts but no lectures. We would offer skilled facilitators, creative techniques and activities, child care and many choices. We would welcome all women as contributors with skills and knowledge to share.

Making the Connections took nearly a year of planning. Many women joined us in making it happen, a few for meagre pay but most as volunteers. For two days, at a beautiful resort on the north shore of Prince Edward Island, more than a hundred women came together to share their ideas and experiences, to laugh and cry and sing and celebrate.

For the five varied women who conceived the gathering, the experience was one of trusting ourselves, trusting the process and trusting the magic created when women gather. How long did we think it would take to change the world? We had few illusions then, fewer now. Seven years later we're each still working — in old and new places, in old and new ways — on issues of violence in which the connections can no longer be hidden.

PS Everything produced for Making the Connections had a "PS" on it, a reminder of our unofficial name: Patriarchy Sucks.

MARCIA BRAUNDY

Carpenter, Coordinator of Women in Trades and Technology
Vallican, British Columbia

I WAS THE FIRST WOMAN in the construction sector of the BC Carpenter's Union. With twelve years at my trade, I have built everything from hospitals to seniors' housing to huge coal silos. My small company has qualified two women apprentices as journey-women. Construction, especially with a large group of people, is some of the most satisfying work I have done.

It's different in my work as an organizer. There I am a catalyst, helping people identify their issues and discovering how to imple-ment solutions. I've organized a national conference on Women in Trades and Technology (WITT) and put together a book on the sub-ject. Currently I am the elected coordinator of the WITT National Network which emerged from that conference.

Exploratory training enables women who have had little experi-ence with carpentry, electronics, mechanics, welding or engineering to make informed career choices. These are occupations that provide real financial recompense as well as the incredible satisfaction of a job well done. The self-esteem gained from competency in using tools can see a woman through many of the challenges in her life, including working in a male-dominated environment.

Men create the environment women encounter in class or on the job. These men often behave inappropriately, many times knowing no other way to be. Kootenay Women in Trades and Technology has developed a seminar for men to assist with the integration of women into technical fields. We work on skill building and prac-tise problem solving. The seminar is based on the concept that everyone has a responsibility for enhancing women's training in and access to trades, technology and blue collar work. When asked by a reporter what it was that I brought to the "brotherhood," my immediate response was "sisterhood!"

KAY MACPHERSON

Peace Activist, Founding Member of Voice of Women
Toronto, Ontario

IN MY WORK FOR PEACE during the last thirty years, I've been called a peacenik, a dupe, a dangerous radical, an impractical idealist, a subversive and lots of other things. In 1964 I was one of a group of women arrested in Paris while peacefully trying to deliver a letter to the Secretary of NATO opposing their plans for a multilateral nuclear force. In 1982, en route to New York to attend a women's conference and the International Peace Rally, I was dumped off the bus by US border officials as an undesirable visitor. Eventually all the press and protests forced the authorities to relent, and I was allowed in, temporarily and depending on my good behaviour. That gave me a chance to be part of the June twelfth rally where I had the experience of a lifetime speaking for Canada to a million people in Central Park.

I am convinced that cooperation, nonviolence and equal rights must form the basis for future society. If we are to survive, we must move away from violence, war and the oppression of one group by another. I believe that a key element in the struggle for the life of our planet will be the participation of women in the decisions that affect us all. Women have a different perspective on things, but this understanding has seldom been used in running societies or solving international problems. Using our own experience, women must work to find new ways of stopping the current drive to self-destruction and of creating a peaceful and constructive world community.

CATHY JONES AS *LOVE MURPHY*

Actor, Playwright; St. John's, Newfoundland

LOVE MURPHY PLAYED a significant role in my life until I had him arrested when he broke a bond and came after me. A change is as good as an arrest, and right now Murph is in the slammer. I hear he's practising sitting meditation and rethinking his life. Good, I say. These are the new old days, and the way Murphy was *modus operandi*-ing just got to be obsolete. Much to his chagrin.

People like and hate Murph for the same reasons. I say let him rot. The male side of me was running the show for too long. I had a dream that a man was running loose and a woman was cowering in fear convinced that he would hurt her. I realized that the man was in me and so was the woman. It was impossible to create with my intuitive, inspired female side hounded by my facilitating male side. I got them together on a beach in my head. She had been blocked by his antics for so long that she was unwilling to trust him, and he had written her off as an emotional mess. I've called a cease-fire and initiated negotiations. I hope that the peace I achieve will manifest itself in relationships full of respect and honesty.

Love Murphy was charming. Swift. A heartbreaker. So was Cathy Jones. Now he and Cathy are both on the road to responsible living. I love Love Murphy, for I have seen the enemy and he is me. In jail they call him Burf. But to me he will always be Love. The Murphy you are looking for is no longer at this address.

THE RAGING GRANNIES

Peace and Environment Activists; Victoria, British Columbia

MARGARET LAURENCE DESCRIBED the threat of nuclear war as "terrorism to which we are all hostage." Women, as bearers and nurturers of life, will not and cannot be apathetic when survival of children and grandchildren is at stake. That is why the Raging Grannies came to be.

At first we appeared on the streets of Victoria as NERTs (Nuclear Emergency Response Teams), wearing hardhats, masks and white coveralls with nuclear radiation symbols sewn on. Our purpose was to alert the community to nuclear powered submarines coming into our port and to the hazards of radiation leakage in the event of an accident.

About a year later it happened. The reality of Chernobyl was too grim for us to carry on with the NERTs exercises. The time had come for grannies to emerge and do what we should do — RAGE for peace, for survival. So out we sallied, dressed in our "best" granny hats, dresses and pink shoes, to try to reach the hearts and minds of people in theatre queues, malls, high schools, anywhere. Armed with satirical verses about nuclear subs in our waters, cruise missile testing overhead and uranium mining underground, we sang our messages of "look what is going on" and "we can change things." Children and grandchildren everywhere must have their time under the sun — to dream, to laugh, to love, to LIVE.

128

TAMARACK AND MOUNTAIN

Founders of The Healing Centre for Women; Ottawa, Ontario

WE CAME TOGETHER in 1981 to form The Healing Centre for Women — A Lesbian Centre of Natural Healing. We have travelled to many parts of Canada listening to women's stories, providing information on healing and exchanging ideas with others doing similar work. Our commitment is to assist women who have been severely harmed by physical, sexual or psychological abuse, as well as to provide opportunities for lesbians to speak openly, free of abuse. In looking for the strength to hear what women have been through and to sort out what we ourselves have been through, we sought out every way of healing we could find and combined what seemed to work.

The Healing Centre and the gatherings that we organize are for women only, at times lesbians only. All of what we have learned and what we teach is gathered from women. We study nutrition to keep alive the herbal remedies that women have always known. We offer a place that is free of all addictive or harmful substances, free from violence of any kind. It is also a sanctuary for wild animals.

Our work is dedicated to those for whom a radical alternative is needed in order to survive, and our strength to continue grows with every woman we see who finds her own strength. We are optimistic in knowing that we are part of a strong network of lesbian healers, each working in her own way.

MARY MACPHERSON

Cook, Union Worker; New Glasgow, Nova Scotia

I'M A WIFE AND THE MOTHER of three active boys. When this picture was taken I was the sole support of my family and a cook at a home for the aged where I worked for thirteen years. I was also president of our union local, in which ninety-five percent of the members were women. I got the local more involved in such groups as the Tearmann Society for Battered Women and the Pictou County Women's Centre.

My involvement in union activities opened a whole new life for me. As president of our local Labour Council and an occasional instructor for my union I taught courses to union members and facilitated workshops for the women's committee of the Nova Scotia Federation of Labour. I enjoyed this teaching immensely, reaching a great number of women and helping them become more involved and assertive. Some went on to positions in various labour organizations.

I feel it is really important to be supportive of other women (our sisters). When I encouraged one woman to run for secretary of our Labour Council, I also showed her how to do the minutes, offered her a ride to the meetings, etc. If we're not willing to give a little time and effort for other women, nobody else will. We've got to find what barriers are holding women back and dismantle them. It's especially difficult for a woman with family responsibilities to achieve the same things men do.

With all my involvement, I make sure that I have time to spend with my family. They are very important in my life. I hope that I can help make this a better world for my kids to grow up in.

YVEL MAZEROLLE

Coordinator, Nouveau Départ (New Start)
Moncton, New Brunswick

I'M 8 YEARS OLD. "The life of a woman is the life of a slave," says my mother. "You, you're going to university; then at least you can choose."

I'm 18 years old. At university the talk is of women's liberation, social injustice, peace. Consciousness-raising groups, demonstrations. Sisterhood flows from our common rage.

I'm 27 years old. I am development officer for Secretary of State, dedicated to the formation of women's groups that exert a social and political influence.

I'm 31 years old. I coordinate a program for the promotion of women within our ministry. We speak of lack of access to top jobs, of child care.

I'm 33 years old. I quit my job, marry and have two children. I am officially a housewife, and I experience directly the isolation and social degradation reserved for that role.

I become coordinator for a course, New Start, which aims to help women re-orient their lives, explore their needs and options. This program assumes that our work — be it volunteer, paid or at home — is always valuable labour.

I'm 39. The model woman never existed; each woman must live her life as best she can. The stereotype of the female super-executive is as insulting as that of the queen of the kitchen.

Women work harder than ever, at more roles. But what is directing the show, materialism or feminism? I have fewer sure answers than I did twenty years ago. I think that the questions are different.

J'ai 8 ans. "La vie d'une femme est une vie d'esclave," dit ma mère. "Toi, tu iras à l'université, et tu pourras au moins choisir."

J'ai 18 ans. A l'université, l'on parle de la libération des femmes, des injustices sociales, de la paix. Groupes de conscientisation, démonstrations. La sororité découle de notre rage commune.

J'ai 27 ans. Je suis agent de développement pour le Secrétariat d'Etat, dévouée à la formation de groupes des femmes qui exerceront une influence sociale et politique.

J'ai 31 ans. Je coordonne le programme de la promotion des femmes au sein de notre ministère. On parle de contraintes d'accès aux postes supérieurs, de la garde des enfants.

J'ai 33 ans. Je quitte mon emploi, me marie, accouche de deux enfants. Je suis officiellement "femme au foyer," et je vis directement l'isolement et la dénigration sociale réservée pour ce rôle. Je deviens coordonnatrice d'un cours, Nouveau Départ, qui veut aider aux femmes à réorienter leur vie, à définir leurs besoins et leurs options. Ce programme présume que notre travail, qu'il soit bénévole, rémunéré, ou au foyer, est toujours du travail valable.

J'ai 39 ans. Il n'existe pas de modèle-type de femme; chacune doit vivre ce qui lui convient du mieux qu'elle peut. Le stéréotype idéal de la super-exécutrice est aussi insultant que celui de la reine du foyer. Les femmes travaillent plus fort que jamais, à plus de rôles. Mais qui dirige la file, le matérialisme ou le féminisme? J'ai moins de réponses assurées qu'il y a vingt ans. Je pense que les questions sont différentes.

ANITA ROBERTS

Assault Prevention Teacher; Vancouver, British Columbia

I TAKE MY BEATEN AND humiliated child-self by the hand. "You are safe now. I know how to protect you." I take my pregnant fifteen-year-old-self in my arms. "You are safe now. I have learned how to say NO." I look into the eyes of my sexually assaulted young woman-self. "You are innocent. It was not your fault."

Together we emerge. Our power shines. I am full of wonder and respect for my spirit's desire to heal. My boy-child is twenty now; I am thirty-six. I teach my Sexual Assault Prevention Program in the Vancouver high schools, exhilarated at being on "the inside" with my deliciously radical ideas. I am a feminist surgeon with access to the inner recesses of the diseased patriarchal body.

I help young women to know the power in their own bodies. I teach them to yell from their bellies. I reveal the injustice of a culture that insists they be as sexually attractive as possible in their dress and behaviour and then accuses them of "asking for it." I struggle to give them creative ways to rethink their conditioning. We examine fashion magazines and rock videos. We work on situations from their own lives — things that have happened to them, things that they fear. We role-play, then rewrite the script using their new assertiveness skills and role-play again. I hear their hidden voices emerge, see their bodies straighten.

My purpose is to empower them, to give them skills and permission to use these skills, to give them a sense of themselves as valuable human beings who do not deserve to be violated. It is an enormous task.

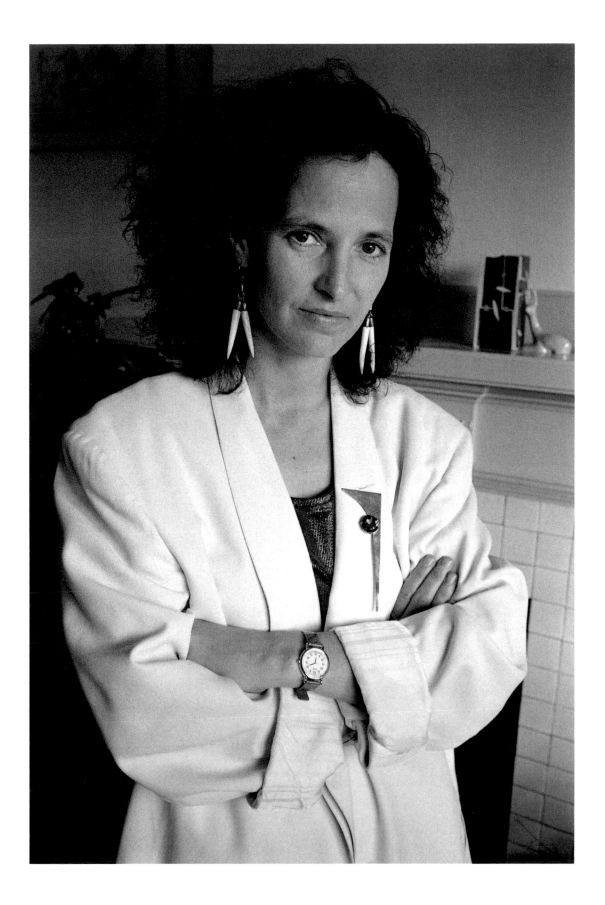

CROSSROADS FOR WOMEN/
CARREFOUR POUR FEMMES

Transition House; Moncton, New Brunswick

OURS IS A SOCIETY that glorifies dominance and violence, portraying it daily on television and in movies — mental food for children and adults alike. Our institutions are based on a hierarchical and adversarial model, and this becomes the model on which many families operate, excusing male behavior exercised in maintaining control. Until very recently churches turned a blind eye to wife abuse, our male-god religions taking the view that man should control woman. It will take generations to make people recognize and eliminate the underlying causes of woman-abuse. In the meantime, as our judicial system and police forces are part of the problem, rather than the help that justice requires, more and more transition houses are needed.

Crossroads for Women opened in 1981 to provide safe shelter, feminist counselling and support to abused women and their children. Our staff are all bilingual; our board is comprised of francophone and anglophone members. We operate as a collective, board and staff having equal say. As there is no director and no boss, our clients have the opportunity to experience a situation where no one is in a dominant position. Half the full time staff hired when we first opened are still with us. The result is a wealth of expertise of great benefit to abused women and their children.

We have no way of knowing how many women's lives Crossroads has saved, but we do know that all the effort has been worthwhile.

Notre société glorifie la violence et la domination. Enfants et adultes sont nourris quotidiennement d'images illustrant ces deux caractéristiques par le biais de la télévision et du cinéma. Nos institutions sont érigées sur un modèle hiérarchique sur lequel se calque la famille et où le comportement de l'homme maintenant le contrôle devient la norme. Jusqu'à récemment l'Eglise fermait les yeux sur la violence faite aux femmes; nos religions adorant le dieu-mâle prêchaient que l'homme devait contrôler la femme. Il faudra encore des générations pour arriver à éliminer les causes de la violence faite aux femmes. Et puisque notre système judiciaire et notre force policière constituent une partie du problème plutôt qu'un renfort pour plus de justice, nous devrons en attendant, augmenter le nombre de maisons de transition.

Carrefour pour femmes fut créé en 1981 pour fournir abri, support et counselling féministe aux femmes abusées et à leurs enfants. Le personnel est bilingue et le conseil d'administration est constitué de membres franco-phones et anglophones. Nous fonctionnons sous forme de collectif donnant au personnel et aux membres du conseil un droit égal aux prises de décisions. Ainsi, sans directeur ni patron, les clientes vivent une expérience où personne n'exerce une position de domination. La moitié du personnel engagé lors de la fondation du Carrefour y travaille toujours et tous savent faire profiter de leur grande compétence.

Si nous ne pouvons compter combien de femmes ont été sauvées par le Carrefour, nous savons en revanche que les efforts fournis n'ont pas été vains.

LE POINT DE RALLIEMENT DES FEMMES HAITIENNES

Montreal, Quebec

PROFESSIONAL WOMEN working mainly in education and health care, we formed The Rallying Point for Haitian Women some twenty years ago. We think it is in women's best interest to unite. We want to encourage other immigrant, Haitian women to break the circle of solitude and to explore new solutions to the problems we face, in order to make a better life in our new land.

Our objectives include mobilizing as many women as possible within the Montreal Haitian community, disseminating information on issues pertaining both to Haitian and non-Haitian women, encouraging the development of solidarity among women, and empowering Haitian women. Besides our annual celebration on International Women's Day, for which we publish a newsletter, we work year round as volunteers in various organizations, trying primarily to respond to the problems facing Haitian women in the community. We support women and children burdened by illiteracy, family violence, exploitation and discrimination. We work for harmonious integration into Quebec society — through education to assure stable employment — and for access to careers traditionally reserved for men. To give women a chance to have their say, we produce a program in Creole for a community radio station.

Dedicated above all to the advancement of Haitian women, we carry out our many tasks in a warm, harmonious atmosphere characterized by friendship.

Nous sommes des professionnelles travaillant notamment en éducation et en santé, et avons fondé Le Point de ralliement des femmes haïtiennes il y a environ vingt ans. Selon nous, les femmes ont intérêt à s'unir pour briser l'isolement et chercher des solutions aux problèmes de dépaysement.

Nos objectifs sont de mobiliser le plus grand nombre de femmes dans la communauté haïtienne de Montréal pour assurer la circulation de l'information sur la condition féminine (des femmes d'ailleurs et d'Haïti), développer de l'esprit de solidarité des femmes et aider la femme haïtienne à se prendre en charge. Nous célébrons la Journée Internationale de la Femme, notamment par la publication d'un bulletin; nous travaillons bénévolement toute l'année avec différents organismes pour essayer de résoudre les problèmes que vit la femme haïtienne dans la communauté. Nous soutenons les femmes et les enfants en butte à l'analphabétisme, la violence familiale, l'exploitation et la discrimination. Nous incitons les femmes à acquérir une formation en vue d'obtenir un emploi stable, d'accéder aux métiers traditionellement réservés aux hommes et de s'intégrer harmonieusement à la société d'accueil. Nous animons une émission en créole à la radio communautaire pour permettre aux femmes de prendre la parole.

Visant avant tout l'épanouissement de la femme haïtienne, nous travaillons dans une atmosphère harmonieuse et chaleureuse, empreinte d'amitié.

EQUAL JUSTICE FOR ALL

Diana Ralph, Linda Schmidt, Margaret Cook
Welfare Rights Group; Saskatoon, Saskatchewan

POVERTY IS A WOMEN'S ISSUE. Most of the poor are women, and most non-poor women are just-a-man-away from poverty. Women are paid between half and two thirds of what men earn. We bear the brunt of child care costs, and no one pays for our own domestic labour. We often work in jobs without pensions or disability insurance. Anti-poverty issues are important women's issues. Jobs, affordable housing, child care and education are basic to women's security. When welfare rates, the minimum wage or unemployment insurance payments rise, it is mainly women who benefit.

Equal Justice for All is a Saskatoon welfare-rights group organized in 1985. Most of us are women, but we also care about men's poverty. We've worked hard to raise welfare rates and to pressure the government to end its punitive, insulting treatment of people on assistance.

Our work has begun to pay off. We won the largest human rights settlement in the history of Canada. We helped to force the last provincial government out of office. We've sparked other welfare rights groups. We helped create a coalition uniting labour and women's groups, aboriginal people, students and farmers.

We still have a long way to go, and we have no regular funding. Everything from office space to writing paper has to be scrounged. All the work is done by dedicated volunteers, most of whom are on welfare themselves. We get tired and frustrated, but we keep working. We have a lot of fun, too, and support one another. We've seen our members grow in confidence and skill through their involvement with the group. As we say in our theme song, "We won't stop until we get equal justice for all."

LISE MOISAN

Lesbian-Feminist Activist; Montreal, Quebec

ALTHOUGH MUCH of the daily work of the women's movement consists of waging exhausting battles to win or save rights and to put in place an endless variety of first-aid services, feminism really is based on the quest for freedom. Hence the concept of liberation, as in The Women's Liberation Movement, or Women's Lib, or even the quaintly derogatory term "libber." Freedom is the radical idea at the heart of feminism and has to do with one's basic posture in life, whatever the degree of oppression, exploitation or victimization one suffers. Essentially, freedom is revealed in our ability to discover and nurture our capacity for freedom itself. Being free does not automatically result from the absence of oppression or victimization any more than being oppressed and victimized necessarily leads one to fight for freedom.

The backlash suffered in the eighties has forced the women's movement to concentrate on preserving earlier gains essential to freedom. But the test of the movement's worth, over the long haul, will be in remaining true to itself and continuing to struggle so that women can cultivate their love of freedom and their ability to achieve it. To succeed where so many other political movements have failed, we must fix our eyes firmly on freedom as *the* goal and not be frightened by what can happen as we begin, individually and collectively, to taste it.

On sait que le plus gros du travail du mouvement des femmes consiste à livrer quotidiennement d'épuisantes batailles pour gagner ou défendre des droits et à mettre sur pied toute une kyrielle de services d'urgence, mais, rappelons-le, le féminisme se fonde sur une quête de liberté. D'où le concept de libération, présent dans l'appellation Mouvement de libération des femmes. Il y a au coeur du féminisme une idée centrale: celle de la liberté. La liberté découle de notre attitude fondamentale dans la vie, et ce, quel que soit le degré d'oppression, d'exploitation ou d'asservissement que l'on subit. Ainsi, elle se manifeste à travers notre capacité de découvrir et de cultiver notre aptitude innée pour la liberté. La liberté ne suppose pas nécessairement une absence d'oppression ou de victimisation, pas plus que d'être opprimée ou victimisée ne garantit qu'on va se battre.

La contre-offensive anti-féministe des années quatre-vingt a obligé le mouvement des femmes à se replier sur une défense des acquis indispensables à toute vie libre. C'est en restant fidèle à lui-même, en continuant de lutter pour que les femmes cultivent leur amour de la liberté et leur potentiel d'êtres libres que le mouvement démontrera sa valeur à long terme. Pour réussir là où tant d'autres mouvements politiques ont échoué, il ne faudra jamais perdre de vue que c'est là notre premier objectif, sans craindre ce qui pourra arriver quand nous goûterons, individuellement et collectivement à notre liberté.

HELEN FOGWILL PORTER

Writer, Activist; St. John's, Newfoundland

As a society we often refuse to see what's staring us in the face. For example, in a book on the subject of serial murderers, the anthropologist-writer gives scant attention to the fact that the killers are all male and their victims all female. He prefers to claim that dissatisfaction with their places in society is what turns those men into murderers. When priest after priest and their colleagues in religion are charged with the sexual abuse of male children, the mainstream media portrays this as a homosexual crime and not as the preying of the powerful upon the weak. It is rarely noted in the press or elsewhere that the abusers are all men.

For years women have been running themselves ragged trying to provide shelter for women and children who have to flee their own homes because they are being beaten and abused by the men in their lives. Why is it taken for granted that this must be solely the responsibility of women?

I don't advocate separation of the sexes. For thirty years I lived happily with a man who saw me as an equal, and my sons enrich my life just as my daughters do. But whether we're talking about the massacre of fourteen women in Montreal by a man who hated feminists or the degrading and cruel objectification of women by male pornographers and the consumers of their products, conditions will never improve while the world continues to overlook the obvious.

THE REGINA TRANSITION WOMEN'S SOCIETY

Regina, Saskatchewan

FOR TEN YEARS, the Regina Transition House had to survive in a home that was too crowded, too dreary and too dark. Painting and wall papering were done only when there was a bit of leftover money. We eagerly accepted donations of used beds and chesterfields, hoping that they would be better than what we had.

The women who came to us had been living with men who constantly told them they were no good, that no other man would ever want them, that they were not worthwhile human beings. Our words would tell them that this was not true, but then we'd guide them up the dingy stairs to a room with one small window and a curtain that didn't fit. The number of beds overpowered the room, and it took some fancy maneuvering to get the beds made. We were embarrassed to have only this to offer.

Now we've moved into a grand old home which makes us proud for what it says to the women who come here. The rich oak, the gigantic fireplaces, the massive windows allowing the sun to stream in make us want to pinch ourselves. For me, these changes bring mixed emotions. It makes me angry that for so many years we had to put up with the worst of the worst, angry that changes happen only when the "powers that be" decide battered women are an up-and-coming-issue. On the other hand, I feel that things do change.

Above all, the message we give to the women who need us comes through. Women do have some power over their own lives. There's still a lot of work to be done, but there is movement and change. That's what we have to keep remembering, for ourselves and for each other, because when we give in to our "victim" roles, we've lost.

GERRY BAILEY

Teacher, Activist; Westerose, Alberta

FIFTY YEARS A FEMINIST has a nice ring. Actually it must be longer than that. My beloved father was a Mountie, and the office and cell were part of our house, so little went on that I missed. By the age of ten I had seen a young girl die of a botched abortion and a baby die of TB in the arms of a young mother. I knew that a father down the street was "doing something" to his daughters and that the girl who cried rape after an attack in a barn was not believed. My father hoped that my generation would be able to eliminate such things. The only place such things have been eliminated is in the memories of those who claim that feminism is the cause of all evil.

In my work as a family-life educator, there have been many highs and lows. In one small town, fundamentalists demanded my program be kept out of the school. To my rescue came a group of feminists who organized a public meeting attended by people from far and wide. A panel of high school students described a class of mine they had attended the year before. They stated that no one had the right to deprive them of that information. One girl said, "Sorry, Mum, but I did have questions that I was too embarrassed to ask you." The mother stood up and replied, "Perhaps Mrs. Bailey could give us classes, too." The program, called "Human Sexuality," was overwhelmingly accepted.

I wish my foresight were as perfect as my hindsight; then I would leave you with a route map. But you have learned to work together for the rights of women, and that's the way to go. Love you.

150

THE ALBERTA COMMITTEE FOR INDIAN RIGHTS FOR INDIAN WOMEN

Philomena Aulotte, Nellie Carlson, Jenny Margetts; Gibbons, Alberta

I WAS IN OTTAWA WHEN Bill C-31, the bill that reinstated Indian women who had married non-Indians, was being discussed in Parliament at the final hour. Outside on the lawn there were about two hundred people, with their drum and singers, that the Indian Association of Alberta had brought to demonstrate against the bill. I was standing there with my son who is half white and half Indian, watching my own relatives and friends demonstrating against us, against Bill C-31. The realization hit me then that we would always be outside. We were winning in Parliament, but we were losing our family, our friends, the welcome back to the reserve.

There was fear, too. After the passage of the bill, the CBC in Ottawa interviewed us and also some of the people from my reserve. When one man was asked what he was going to do now that the women could return to the reserve, he smiled and said that he was going to use "Judge Colt." When we realized he was talking about guns, about the *Colt*, we were so shocked we didn't know what to say.

It's years since the passage of Bill C-31, but even now the chiefs of Alberta refuse to let women move back to the reserves. Those chiefs are warring against their own people, their own women and those women's children. They need to get educated and learn who is the real enemy in the survival of our people.

ANGELA MILES

Feminist Theorist, Educator; Toronto, Ontario

I HAVE BEEN CONCERNED WITH ISSUES of social justice ever since my teenage years and was active for a long while in male-dominated politics. When I did become a feminist, it was a "conversion experience," transforming my relationship to myself, to women, to the world and to political activism.

Feminism came first as a breathtaking awareness that I share a condition with other women. This made it possible for me to see that as women we could identify our own interests, trust our own experience and name the world from our own point of view. Taking this power involved displacing men from the centre of my thinking and my world view. This enormous shift in perspective was a deeply liberating experience. I realized that my strengths connected me to rather than separated me from other women and that women are strong *because* we are women, not in spite of it. Our very marginality to all structures of power allows us to see and to say that the Emperor has no clothes.

This was nothing less than my rebirth as a whole person. With hindsight I could see that I had been "allowed" to participate "equally" in male-defined politics on condition that I denied my femaleness in the name of an abstract, ungendered personhood that was, nevertheless, male. Feminism was the healing of this debilitating split.

For me the celebration of women is the radical core of feminist politics, which is as much about women's strength as women's oppression. The affirmation of women's lives and skills is deeply energizing to women raised in a misogynist world which devalues and trivializes us. Feminism provides a basis on which we can go beyond struggling to be accepted as one of the boys in their world and their game to challenging the very rules of the game and the values and structures of their world. So, for me, feminism represents a broadening and deepening of progressive struggle in general.

CHRIS CLARK

Civil Servant, Feminist Activist; Winnipeg, Manitoba

I HAVE DEVELOPED SEVERAL operating techniques during my life: keep it simple, have fun, do three things at once, be patient, start wherever you are and do whatever you can. It is not easy to change the world. We do it a bit at a time and mostly in our own little areas.

The Same Damn Bunch, created in 1975, is a good example of this. We are a few women who will drop everything and do whatever is needed at a particular moment, without meetings, agendas or structure. We organized the first Canadian Women's Cultural and Music Festival in Winnipeg. We became the Society for Demolishing Barriers when we set up a scholarship for women entering nontraditional areas of training. We sponsored *Prairie Spirits*, a record of three Manitoba women singing their songs. We set up a housing co-op in the recognition that most women face poverty in their older years and need security of shelter and a supportive community. We have retreats, dinners, movie discussions; we print calendars and handbooks; and always we have fun, celebrate women and work to change the world.

We have suffered so long with a one-sided view; to see the world as a whole and not as a half is a very exciting prospect. Why not change the decision-making system? Let's cut the number of constituencies in half and in every one allow each party to run two candidates — one male and one female. Immediately we would have fifty percent women in all levels of government, all elected democratically. Then let's see how our priorities change.

When I look at my granddaughter I see great hope. She is so connected with people, so caring and full of fun. What more can we hope for? Nellie McClung was right — don't apologize, don't explain, just get it done, and let them howl!

GIRLS ARE PEOPLE (GAP)

Brandon, Manitoba

WHEN WE WERE ABOUT NINE OR TEN we hung around together because our mothers were friends. We spent our time playing games, running about at twilight, drawing, writing stories. We grew up reading feminist folk tales and admiring creative, courageous women who were great thinkers and adventurers. In our childhood games we became those women, women who were not decorations or prizes to be won but central. Such women existed in our time spent together, but they were missing elsewhere. We couldn't understand why most girls wanted to be princesses while we admired the Amazons. Girls Are People was born.

We held regular meetings in the office of the Manitoba Action Committee on the Status of Women. At each meeting we discussed a certain theme or had a specific goal. Our first major project was writing and performing a play about the prairie suffrage movement. We learned to operate video equipment. We went to feminist plays and concerts and to solstice parties with our moms. We marched annually at Take Back the Night events. When one of us started to menstruate, we had a party where we sat in a circle, passing a red candle from friend to friend, sharing our thoughts about periods and about being young women.

Being in Girls Are People was about feeling secure in our ideas and speaking out for change. We're older now than when this picture was made. It's been a while since we've met as a group. We're growing up and meeting the kind of creative and courageous women we played at being in our childhood games. We look forward to the day when all the GAP members can get together again to talk about our thoughts and adventures, this time as women.

NICOLE BROSSARD

Writer; Montreal, Quebec

SINCE IN PRINCIPLE language belongs to everyone, we are entitled to reappropriate it by taking the initiative to intervene when it gives the impression of closing itself off and when our desire clashes with common usage. Somehow feminist consciousness and lesbian emotion incite us to process reality and fiction in such a way that we have no choice but to reinvent language. The reinvented language is a language in which every woman can recognize herself, find her dignity, hear the modulated sounds of her voice. But the reinvented language is above all an unedited space in which the unthought of the world suddenly takes the form of evidence.

In the necessity and the desire to reinvent the language there is certainly an intention of happiness, a utopic thrust, a serious responsibility. It is because I feel profoundly each in me that I continue my course of writing. Voyage without end, writing is what always comes back to seek me out in order to distance death and stupidity, fear and violence. Writing never lets me forget that if life has a meaning, somewhere, it is in what we invent with our lives, with the aura of several words which, within us, form sequences of truth. I have always thought that the word beauty is related to the word desire. There are words which, like the body, are irreducible: *to write* **I am a woman** *is full of consequences.*

C'est parce que, en principe, la langue appartient à tout le monde qu'à juste titre nous nous la réapproprions en prenant l'initiative d'intervenir quand elle donne l'impression de se clore et que notre désir se heurte à l'usage. Quelque part, le travail, le traitement de la réalité et de la fiction auquel nous oblige la conscience féministe, auquel nous initient l'imaginaire et l'expérience lesbienne, ce travail nous incite à réinventer la langue. La langue réinventée, c'est une langue dans laquelle chaque femme peut se reconnaître, trouver sa dignité, entendre les sons modulés de sa voix. Mais la langue réinventée, c'est surtout un espace inédit ou l'impensée du monde prend forme soudain comme une évidence.

Il y a certainement dans la nécessité et le désir de réinventer la langue, une intention de bonheur, une trame utopique, une sérieuse responsabilité. C'est parce que je ressens profondément l'une et l'autre en moi que je continue mon parcours d'écriture. Voyage sans fin, l'écriture est ce qui toujours revient me chercher afin d'éloigner la mort et la bêtise, la peur et la violence. L'écriture ne me permet jamais d'oublier que si la vie a un sens, quelque part, il est dans celui que nous inventons à même nos vies, à même l'aura de quelques mots qui, en nous, forment des séquences de vérité. J'ai toujours pensé que le mot beauté s'apparentait au mot désir. Il y a des mots qui, comme le corps, sont incontournables: écrire *je suis une femme* est plein de conséquences.

GAIL GELTNER

Graphic Artist; Toronto, Ontario

CONTAINED WITHIN THIS PHOTOGRAPH are the objects of my earliest memory — paper, paintbrush, table. My four-year-old self moves determinedly across an expanse of sunlit floor towards a table strewn with brushes and large sheets of paper. In another part of the room a group of children gather around a teacher. Lifting the brush, I become that most solemn of creatures, a child at play.

I've spent most of my working life poised before a rectangle of paper, struggling, faltering, searching, in joy and in misery peering into that space where all things can coexist. The work is solitary, but the audience is felt and is necessary for completion of the action begun on the page.

I was introduced to the emerging feminist literature in the early seventies when a feminist press asked me to illustrate a book on women and work. The material was startling. Following one book to another, I acquired an overview of women's role in the social movements for civil rights, racial equality, labour reform. This experience allowed me to see my own work as part of a tradition. I joined others in boisterous discussion and in organizing feminist art exhibitions, housing co-ops and environmental conferences. Such involvements continue to carry me into widening circles of connection and commitment.

As a child I imagined I might someday speak with each person in the world. A peculiar desire for such a shy and silent child. Now the peoples of the world are pressed into desperate flight, and life everywhere is threatened. We are all together and must speak with one another. What will we say? What will we do ?

162

WOMEN'S SUPPORT GROUP

Crowbush, Prince Edward Island

WE AFFIRM EACH OTHER. We nurture, respect and challenge each other. That's what our support group is all about. We are comforted by the reliability of ritual, by the specific ways we are within the group. Our need for each other is highlighted by our Island isolation. Mainland women seem so far away. Our commitment is to work things out — class divisions, racism, homophobia, whatever — after all, we are all we have.

We come together to create a special space where our woman-voices can be heard: on a six a.m. beach with waves lapping the red sand and the sun cracking the morning sky; or in a wintry country kitchen with woodstove, candles, voices raised in song and a friendly dog snoring nearby; or beside a grove of Island spruce trees with lupins and early ladyslippers.

We play music, read poetry, eat together, laugh, roar and chant. We share hopes and dreams. Confidentiality is a given, our trust built over time. Within each circle the focus is different — healing, birth, transition, commitment and all the in-betweens of women's lives. Lovers come and go; babies are carried and born; houses are built; journeys (physical and spiritual) are taken. We are rich with shared experience.

DOROTHY LIVESAY

Poet; Victoria, British Columbia

The woman I am
is not what you see
I'm not just bones
and crockery

the woman I am
knew love and hate
hating the chains
that parents make

longing that love
might set men free
yet hold them fast
in loyalty

the woman I am
is not what you see
move over love
make room for me

AFTERWORD

Pamela Harris

UNDERTAKING A LARGE PROJECT is like beginning a journey. You may know where you want to go and how you hope to get there, but in the end the event defines itself. *Faces of Feminism* was a journey that took many years. My aim was to make a portrait series recording the Canadian women's movement and to do this in a way that would not diminish the breadth of the subject. During the time I worked on the project, I also raised a family, moved house, did some teaching and undertook other photographic work, but *Faces of Feminism* was always present. Like the women's movement itself, it was a process.

It's a sunny afternoon in 1981. On a tiny back porch glassed in from the raw March air, Mary O'Brien is holding forth over a cup of tea. We've just made a portrait for the dust-jacket of her new book, "The Politics of Reproduction." I enjoy her wit as the Scottish voice and warm sunlight flow over me. "What a good thing it would be," I think, "to make portraits of other women who are revisioning the world, changing the way we can live our lives." Looking back now, it seems appropriate that Mary, a former midwife, was present at the birth of that idea.

What is history but the conqueror's story, carrying the conqueror's values and world view? Historically, what we do or know as women has been written on sand and washed away by regular tides of patriarchal revision. Our female experiences have been marginalized and distorted for thousands of years. Like others who don't fit the dominant mold, we must keep our own histories, or we will lose them. We need to keep these histories in our own way, as well, for how we record ourselves reveals and transmits our values. There are many methods of keeping track of ourselves; making pictures and collecting stories is one of them.

It's 1984, Toronto's 150th birthday. Funding had been awarded for ten photographic documentations of the city, including my series on the Toronto feminist community. At the opening of the group exhibition, my daughters and their friends cluster noisily around the food, chins just reaching table height. In my alcove, many of the women I photographed

169

enjoy this good excuse for a gathering. Sometimes their faces surprise me,
for I have come to visualize them as they appear in the photographs.

Spring of '85. A fat envelope arrives from The Canada Council,
where I've applied for funds to make feminist portraits coast to coast. I
know by the size of the packet that it must be a "yes," and I am both
thrilled and horrified. "Now I'm actually going to do it!" Months later,
while I research the national project, the Toronto portraits are being
shown at a district library. A distraught librarian calls to say that an
angry patron has smashed one of the pieces to the ground. I know before
she names it which it will have been — the image and words of the
Canadian Abortion Rights Action League. "Well," I think, "at least they're
reading the texts."

A representation of the feminist community calls for more than
faces on a wall; it needs analysis and memory. For *Faces of Feminism*
I asked the women I photographed to write — as feminists —
about their lives, work or deepest concerns. Each would choose her
own subject and write in her own voice. Image and text would
form a partnership. My job would be to include diverse women
who could raise a variety of issues, to support them in the task of
writing and, finally, to edit their words. But that was much later.
First I had to figure out whom and where to photograph.

Morning. A letter arrives. I get mail from all over the country now,
almost all from women I have never met. This time someone has passed
on one of my letters to Diane Duggan in St. John's, Newfoundland. She
sends a list of women from across Canada and urges me to include
Eunadie Johnson in Thompson, northern Manitoba. I sit in a closet-sized
study in Toronto, holding a letter from a woman I don't know in a far
corner of Canada who is sending me to photograph another woman I
don't know in another corner of the country. I am in the middle of a web
being spun out with stamps, ink and good will. It's exciting but also
scarey. I will owe everyone so much.

In *Faces of Feminism* I wanted, as far as I could, to let the
women's community define itself. I wanted the process to be a feminist one. I would work from the bottom up and be responsive to
what I found. Since feminists are found in many places, I would try
to include women in small towns and rural environments as well as
in cities. I would photograph groups and individuals, women of
differing ages, races, classes, professions, sexual preference and so

forth. I would cast a wide net. To begin, I sent a lot of letters to widening circles of women, explaining my project and asking for names and advice, filling boxes with file cards as the network grew.

Faces of Feminism not only was defined by the feminist community; it was also nurtured. Women I had never met took time to advise me, to organize appointments, to help me get around, to make me feel at home, to put me up (and to put up with me), to be — in the fullest sense of the word — sisterly. Some of these women appear in the final collection; many do not. Yet all of them have a presence in the project, for it was built with their aid. I felt at times as if I were being handed across the country bodily, from woman to woman, all of them intent that I get the job done.

I turn into a lane leading to a silk-grey, Nova Scotia barn. I'm feeling shy, as always before meeting someone. Jane Morrigan takes me to the barn where her dairy herd waits for the evening milking. The line of cows face a line of eye-level mirrors and a mural of trees, clouds, animals. They have names like Georgia O'Keefe, Emma Goldman and Mary Two-Axe Earley. "Thank you, Emma; thank you, Pandora"; Jane acknowledges each milking. She talks about her work at a nearby women's centre and about her animals. I am reminded that photography has many rewards — friendship, being a fly on the wall, being welcomed where otherwise you might never enter.

Learning about a province took months, though the photographing that resulted there was concentrated into a few weeks. Researching and making portraits across the country was done over five years. Once many suggestions from a province were in hand, I would confer with a variety of local women — by letter and telephone — to select a workable number and a balanced group. In British Columbia, for example, I started with the names of two women, developed a nineteen-page, computerized list and chose from that about forty-five subjects. But for all the research and pre-arrangements, some of my favorite pictures came as gifts.

It's night-time, November, about thirty below. I'm in a tiny rented car, driving north to Minnedosa, Manitoba to photograph a group of women setting up a rural crisis line. I turn onto a small road. There are no houses to be seen. I am tired from a long day of talking and photographing, nervous that I am late for this last group that awaits me. The road becomes deep with snow, too narrow for turning, just ruts with a hump of frozen

grasses scraping the underside of the car. Far away, one or two lights glim-
mer. That was definitely the wrong turn, and if I get stuck, I freeze. The
snow deepens; the ruts narrow till, finally, they swerve into a space
packed hard enough for me to turn and escape.

I don't do justice that evening to the Minnedosa support group. But I
meet a wheat farmer, Cindy Murray, whom I photograph the next day
before driving to my appointment in Winnipeg. I make another stop, as
well, for I have been asking about midwives: "Does anyone know any
feminist midwives?" "There's Darlene Birch; she used to live in St.
Eustache. Call from the gas station at the second set of lights." The wheat
farmer and the midwife end up in the collection while the carefully
researched and scheduled women I photographed before and after them do
not.

How to describe this mix of endless planning and random response? *Faces of Feminism* is a gathering, a sampling, a core extracted from many layers of rock. It is not a who's-who. There are some recognizable names, but many of the women recorded here are known only within their own communities. They come in many guises and hold divergent points of view, but they share a commitment to the difficult process of reshaping human society beyond the confines of patriarchy. That they are so various and so uncommonly commonplace reminds us of a central truth — that feminists are everywhere and can be any woman.

Too often we are presented with a portrait of feminism that has been cast in a patriarchal mold and presents "the movers and shakers," the stars. Feeding on such impressions, we draw some sustenance from the model offered of women's accomplishments. But this version of feminism can also weaken us, making us feel that they, the heralded ones, are other, while we, unheralded, are merely living our lives—being sisterly to our co-workers or supporting the family planning clinic or trying to raise children in a non-sexist way. Such a separation of us and them erodes our sense of connection and diminishes what the women's movement can be.

Real history is not the few names haloed by officialdom but all the private energies collectively spent. Potentially, each woman has her own point of connection with feminism, her own contribution to make, growing from the experience and passion that belong to her. Appreciating and supporting this potential in ourselves and in one another gives us energy and power.

172

1989. The photographing is done. The gallery that began the project with seed money in 1984 has called to propose a show. I must select images and track down missing texts. I call Louky Bersianik. Her picture, taken in May, reflects her warmth and the friendliness of our meeting. She writes her text in late December after the Montreal massacre, and her anger steams off the page — between image and text a compelling tension.

Some women write a few lines; others send small essays. I try to fit the pieces into the allotted space while leaving their individuality intact. There are so many different chemistries between us, woman to woman, image to text. Typing the texts into the computer and editing them, I feel I am still in conversation; I hear the rhythms of different voices. Sometimes, when the radio is on, I really do hear a familiar voice and recognize it as belonging to one of the women I have photographed. Alone in my workroom, I feel their companionship.

Like a performer trying to keep all the balls in the air, I juggled many criteria in editing the exhibition and later the book. I considered the quality of the photographs and texts, the variety of provinces, ages, races, personal types and topics discussed, whether the images were of groups or individuals. Nervously I set aside my photographer's ego, giving the writing equal weight, maintaining the balance of face and voice. The choices were painful as from hundreds I selected several dozen. Behind every woman or group that I could include were so many others, just as active, just as interesting.

The women who appear in this collection are representatives of a wide constituency. You cannot predict where you will find such women. Nor are they monolithic in their point of view, for the women's movement is an evolving process dependent on the push and pull of many perspectives. So, to understand feminism one must look at the diversity of women who espouse it, live it and thereby create it.

Hanging in the gallery, the pictures form a circle of women. At the opening, I think of these women as part of the party. There are many emotions. I am relieved to see the work framed and on the walls. Friends are happy. One viewer cannot speak for tears. Two young men tell me they feel empowered by the collection. An old woman in blue sneakers spends hours reading all the texts. My children and their friends write silly notes in the comment book and spill their sodas.

A documentary project is only as meaningful as the use it gets, and an exhibition is seen by relatively few. Even on the walls of the gallery, *Faces of Feminism* looked like a book, which is what I meant it to be. Of the few publishers that came to look, two got interested and talked seriously about costs and numbers; but one died, and the other went out of business. Rescue came, ultimately, from the women at Second Story Press who decided to publish the collection on the understanding that we would first find the money needed to reproduce so many photographs.

Over the following months we learned about fundraising and searched for support. But we raised no money until shown the way by the very women I had photographed. "Just do it," came one woman's ringing precept. "Sell it in advance," urged another friend. Encouraged by the thought of feminist artists who had taken this route, we made up flyers and began to sell sponsorships, reaching out across the country. The book of *Faces of Feminism* would be made possible by the same feminist networking process on which the entire project had been built.

❧

The story is about energy. I gathered the energy that propelled this journey from friends who helped me, from the many women who wrote and advised me, from the groups that funded me, from the patience of my family as I carried out an endless task. I used that energy as I planned, travelled and photographed. I found it again in the good conversations, the friendships, the hospitality I received on my journeys. I gave it out by pushing on with the project; I got it back when women sent me their writing, when the work was shown, when viewers responded to the exhibition. I spent it trying to get the material published; I received it when Second Story Press agreed to undertake the publication and when our sponsors and donors gave their support. I caught it from the women I met – diverse, specific, thoughtful, energetic – and tried to put it into this book. Now the energy that comes from these women on these pages is yours, to catch and use. That's what empowerment is all about.

Sponsors

LIST OF SPONSORS

LOUISE ABBOTT ❦ B. AGAR ❦ DENISE AINSWORTH
DIANE AITKEN ❦ MILNOR ALEXANDER ❦ PAUL C.
ANDERSEN ❦ AIMÉE ANDERSON ❦ BARBARA ANDERSON
SUSAN ANTHONY ❦ ANTIGONISH WOMEN'S ASSOCIATION
LINDA & WALTER ARD ❦ LOUISE ARDENNE ❦ JANE
ARONSON ❦ M. ASSHETON-SMITH ❦ LOUISE AZZARELLO
GERRY BAILEY ❦ L. AMANDA BAILEY ❦ JILL R. BAIRD
DONNA BAPTIST ❦ ROSEMARIE BAHR ❦ BECKY
BARRETT, MLA ❦ JOY ADAMS BAUER ❦ MCBEAU BECHER
LEAH ERNA BECK ❦ *IN MEMORY OF* SHIRLEY BEKAERT
BEATRICE BIBBY ❦ V. I. BIRSS ❦ THE BISHOP STRACHAN
SCHOOL ❦ MURIEL BISHOP ❦ *IN MEMORY OF*
AGNES EMILY BANNINGER BLAIN ❦ SARA BLAKE ❦ JUDY
BLANKENSHIP ❦ CAROL BLENKIN ❦ THE BOARD OF
EDUCATION, CITY OF TORONTO ❦ JULIE BOGHARDT
ELIZABETH BOHNEN ❦ MARLENE BOKSHOWAN
DR. DAVID E. BOND ❦ ANNE BORCHARDT ❦ PATTY
BOSSORT ❦ PAULA T. BOURNE ❦ ANNE BOWERBANK
KATE BRAID ❦ CYNTHIA LEAVENS BRANNAN ❦ MARCIA
BRAUNDY ❦ ANGELA BRAYHAM ❦ HEATHER BRENNEMAN
LINDA BRONFMAN ❦ LAURIE BROWN ❦ SUSAN BROWN
LIZ BURGE ❦ REBECCA BURKE ❦ ANNE BUTLER ❦ CARAL
JUNE CALLWOOD ❦ ALLISON D. CAMPBELL ❦ CARLETON
UNIVERSITY WOMEN'S CENTRE COLLECTIVE ❦ CARREFOUR
POUR FEMMES/CROSSROADS FOR WOMEN ❦ ALISON CARTER
CHRISTINE CECI ❦ BARBARA ELLEN CENTER ❦ CHRIS CLARK
MARG CLARK ❦ MARGARET CLARK ❦ JANINE O'LEARY
COBB ❦ LINDA COLBOURNE ❦ HOLLY COLE
MURIEL COLLINS ❦ COMITÉ PERMANENT SUR LE STATUT DE LA
FEMME, SECRÉTARIAT GÉNÉRAL, UNIVERSITÉ DE MONTRÉAL
CORNISH ADVOCATES ❦ BRENDA COUCH ❦ REBECCA
COULTER ❦ JUDITH CRAWLEY ❦ CUPE LOCAL 2204
KATHY DAHL ❦ HÉLÈNE DAVID ❦ JACQUELINE
MACGREGOR DAVIES ❦ BOB DAVIS ❦ SUSAN DE ROSA
ANNE-MARIE DELOREY ❦ DEPARTMENT OF WOMEN'S
STUDIES, CARLETON UNIVERSITY ❦ MARGARET DEMPSEY
LINDA DENNING ❦ HELEN L. DERBYSHIRE
DES ACTION CANADA ❦ H. DEVOR ❦ JUDY DIBUS
EMMA DICKSON ❦ MARTY DOLIN ❦ DR. E. L. DONALDSON
WENDY DONNER ❦ KIMBERLEY DOUCET ❦ SHEILAH
MACKINNON DROVER ❦ MARTHA DUGAN
EAST END LITERACY, TORONTO ❦ DR. MARGRIT EICHLER

NANCY ELLARD ❦ ANNE ELLIOTT ❦ SHIRLEY JANE ENDICOTT
MARIA ERIKSEN ❦ LINDA M. ERVIN ❦ EXECUTIVE COUNCIL
OFFICE WOMEN'S DIRECTORATE, GOVERNMENT OF THE YUKON
NICOLA HO FATT ❦ LISA B. FELDBERG ❦ LORNA RAPSON
FERGUSON ❦ SHELLEY FINSON ❦ BARB FLEMINGTON
JOYCE FORBES ❦ ANNE ROCHON FORD ❦ HENRIETTE
ROCHON FORD ❦ FRIEDA FORMAN ❦ RICHARD FOXTON
MAYANN FRANCIS ❦ URSULA FRANKLIN ❦ LYNN FRASER
V. FRENKEL ❦ BONNIE FUGLE ❦ JULIE GALANT ❦ DORIS
GALLAGHER ❦ FRAN GALLAGHER-SHUEBROOK ❦ LEANNE
GANES ❦ LYNN GAUDET ❦ GAIL GELTNER ❦ GENDER
ISSUES RESOURCE CENTRE, BROCK UNIVERSITY STUDENTS'
UNION ❦ CAROLE GERSON ❦ JANINE GIBSON
DR. MARGARET GILLETT ❦ SUZANNE GIRARD ❦ RUTH &
VERNE GLEASON ❦ DANIELLE GODIN ❦ RENAE BARLOW &
JODI GOLDING ❦ MARIA GOMES ❦ TERESA GONZALEZ
MARY GORDON ❦ SUSAN GOTTHEIL ❦ TERAL GRAY
FIONA GREEN ❦ GLORIA GREENFIELD ❦ DONNA
GRESCHNER ❦ VIRGINIA R. GRIFFIN ❦ SUE GRIGGS
EUNICE DE GRUCHY ❦ MARY GUNN ❦ LOUISE HAGER
LYNDA HAMILTON ❦ JANICE HANDFORD ❦ CRAIG & DONNA
HARRIS ❦ MARJORIE HARRIS ❦ FLORENCE & JOHN HARRIS
IRENE HEAMAN ❦ HELEN HENGEL ❦ MARTA HERBERTSON
HESTIA HOUSE ❦ CHRISTINE HIGGINS ❦ DENISE
HILDEBRAND ❦ SHELLY HILDITCH ❦ GAIL HILYER
BARBARA SCOTT HOBBS ❦ SUSAN CLOSE & RICHARD HOLDEN
THADDEUS HOLOWNIA ❦ ANNE HOUTMAN ❦ SANDRA
HRYCHUK ❦ JUDY HUBER ❦ ELIZABETH HUDDLE
DEBORAH HUDSON ❦ LINDA S. HUI ❦ DONNA HUNTER
PAT HUNTER ❦ SUE INGLIS ❦ KATE INMAN ❦ LIZ INMAN
MARY JACKMAN ❦ NANCY JACKMAN ❦ DONNA JACQUES -
ALLAN ❦ ROSE JANSON ❦ KARIN JASPER ❦ CHRISTINE
JOHNSON ❦ ARTA JOHNSON ❦ REBECCA JOHNSON
WAVIE JOHNSON ❦ ANN JONES ❦ BRIAN & JUDY JONES
MOON JOYCE ❦ SYLVIA M. KAJIURA ❦ MARLYN A. KANE
LYNN KEARNEY ❦ MARION KERANS ❦ PATRICIA KENNY
DR. MARY KEYES ❦ DR. J.S. KEYSTONE ❦ SUSIE KING
BONNIE KLEIN ❦ JOANNE KOHOUT ❦ KRYS KOLACZ
GERALDINE KORBA ❦ JOAN KOTARSKI ❦ CAROLYN KREBS
DR. SIMON KREINDLER ❦ ELLEN KRUGER ❦ LABOUR
COLLEGE OF CANADA ❦ LAKEHEAD UNIVERSITY LIBRARY
JEANNE LANCE ❦ CAROL LANE ❦ PATRICIA LANE ❦ SUSAN

M. Langley ❦ Olive Lawson ❦ Lois Laycraft ❦ Rita Lécuyer ❦ Julie Anne Le Gras ❦ Anne Le Rougetel ❦ Sandi Kirby & Amanda Le Rougetel ❦ Helen Levine ❦ R. Tamara Levine ❦ Nancy Lewis ❦ Suzanne Lewis ❦ Deborah Ann Light ❦ Doreen Lindsay ❦ Ottie Lockey ❦ Karen M. Lodl ❦ Linda Macdonald ❦ Nancy C. Macdonald ❦ G.G. MacFarlane ❦ Claire Mackay ❦ A. Jean MacKenzie ❦ Dortohy MacKeracher ❦ Jean MacNaughton ❦ Kathleen Macpherson ❦ Lillian Nakamura Maguire ❦ Kathleen Mahoney ❦ Sally Mahood ❦ Diana Majury ❦ Cheryl Malmo ❦ Ruth Mandel ❦ Ann Manicom ❦ Elizabeth Markon ❦ Del Marlow ❦ H.J. Maroney ❦ Kay Marshall ❦ Fraidie Martz ❦ Vandra Masemann ❦ Dorine Mazerolle ❦ Christina McCall ❦ Sandra McCrone ❦ S.J. McCullagh ❦ Donna McDonagh ❦ Susan McDonald ❦ Thelma McGillivray ❦ Joan S. McKee ❦ Carol McKeen ❦ Sylvia McKinlay ❦ Christine McLeod ❦ Wilson McLeod ❦ Diane McMahon ❦ Yasmine Mehmet ❦ Joan Meister ❦ Elizabeth Menzies ❦ Angela Miles ❦ Andrea Milinkovich ❦ Joan Miller ❦ Ruth Miller ❦ Mr. & Mrs. David Mirvish ❦ Penni Mitchell ❦ Patti Moore ❦ Sky Blue Mary Morin ❦ Cathy Morocco ❦ Catherine Hughes & Jane Morrigan ❦ Martha Muzychka ❦ Lucia Nixon ❦ Myra Novogrodsky ❦ Ann Nowlan ❦ Mary O'Brien ❦ Susan O'Donnell ❦ Ontario Arts Council ❦ Oshawa Durham Rape Crisis Centre ❦ Elsie Paget ❦ Carmen Paquette ❦ Carol Jean Pardoe ❦ Madeleine Parent ❦ Joan Parrish ❦ Karen Patterson ❦ PEI Advisory Council on the Status of Women ❦ Addie Penner ❦ Beth Percival ❦ Susan Perly ❦ Rosanne Perron ❦ M. Ruth Pickering ❦ Vincenzo Pietropaolo ❦ Bonnie Plunkett ❦ "From A Woman Poet" ❦ Beth Pollock ❦ Joanne Prindiville ❦ Jerilynn C. Prior ❦ Bernice Prosser ❦ Provincial Women's Committee, Ontario Public Service Employees Union ❦ Diana Ralph ❦ Dr. Ruth S. Ralph ❦ L. Pauline Rankin ❦ Charlene Reader ❦ Judy Rebick ❦ Donna E. Reid ❦ Satu Repo ❦ Ruby Reske-Naurocki ❦ Richmond Women's Resource Centre ❦ Dr. June Mills & Joe Ridel ❦ Jillian Ridington ❦ Kerry Rittich ❦ Anita Roberts ❦ Lana Lockyer Robinson ❦ Kristen Meridel Robinson ❦ Kerstin Roger ❦ Brian MacLeod Rogers ❦ Janet Rogers ❦ Mary K. Rombout ❦ Sharon Rona ❦ Rheta Rosen ❦ Mary Rowles ❦ Carol E. Rowntree ❦ Agnes Roy ❦ Joan Ryan ❦ June Sale ❦ Lois Sapsford ❦ Saskatchewan Christian Feminist Network ❦ Saskatchewan Education, Northern Division ❦ Wendy Scholefield ❦ Scugog Rape Crisis Centre ❦ Pat Seebach ❦ Janka Seydegart ❦ Marsha Sfeir ❦ Michelle Shrott ❦ Kimberly Simcoe ❦ Evanna Simpson ❦ Sam Simpson ❦ Marian Smith ❦ Donna E. Smyth ❦ Joanne Snyder ❦ Susan J. Sorensen ❦ Judy Stanleigh ❦ Bill Stapleton ❦ Randa Stewart ❦ Colleen Stickle ❦ Deborah Stienstra ❦ Bonnelle Strickling ❦ Beverly Suek ❦ Roberta Sutherland Tanis ❦ Gladys Tallman ❦ Cindy Talock ❦ Charlene Thacker ❦ Gillian Thomas ❦ Gordon W. Tisdall ❦ Terry E. Toews ❦ The Rev. Ann E. Tottenham ❦ Susan Traill ❦ Danielle Marie Trinque ❦ Alexandra Keir & Donna Truesdale ❦ Joann Trypuc ❦ Verna Turner ❦ Abby Ulmer ❦ Vancouver Women's Bookstore ❦ Bernadette Vangool ❦ Jill Vickers ❦ Pat Vickers ❦ Velma Vosper ❦ Jennifer Waelti-Walters ❦ Larry Wahl ❦ Elizabeth Cusack Walsh ❦ Amy Kotkin Warner ❦ Waterloo Region R.C.S. School Board ❦ Lisa Weintraub ❦ Jennifer Welsh ❦ Susan Wendell ❦ West Kootenay Women's Association ❦ Diana R. Wetmore ❦ Judy Whalen ❦ Maribell White ❦ Marilyn Whiteley ❦ Renate Wickens-Feldman ❦ Margaret Wiesenberg ❦ Terre Flower & Carolyn Wilkinson ❦ Wendy Williams ❦ Kathlene R. Willing ❦ Jean Wilson ❦ Jeri Wine Women's Bookstop ❦ Women's Centre, University of Winnipeg Students' Association ❦ Women's Collective & Resource Centre, University of Calgary ❦ Women's Directorate, Government of the Yukon ❦ Women's Health Clinic, Winnipeg ❦ Women's Resource Centre Hay River, NWT ❦ Women's Studies Program, University of Victoria ❦ Women's Studies Programme, Atkinson College ❦ Women's Studies Programme, Dalhousie University ❦ Working for Women, Saskatoon ❦ Janet M. Wood ❦ Yellowknife Public Library ❦ Marian Yeo ❦ Shannon Zech

INDEX AND INFORMATION

Women representing groups are listed in order from left to right.

KAY MACPHERSON, *page 124.*
Peace Activist, Founding Member of Voice of Women,
Toronto, Ontario, 1984.

MARY MACPHERSON, *page 132.*
Cook, Union Worker; New Glasgow, Nova Scotia, 1985.

MAKING THE CONNECTIONS, *page 120.*
Beth Percival, Lyle Brehaut, Julie Dodd, Margaret Ashford,
Jill Lightwood; Brackley Beach, Prince Edward Island, 1986.

JUDY MARCHAND, *page 38.*
With Adrienne; Activist, Potter; Brandon, Manitoba, 1985.

YVEL MAZEROLLE, *page 134.*
With Julien; Coordinator, Nouveau Départ (New Start);
Moncton, New Brunswick, 1989.

JOAN MEISTER AND SHIRLEY MASUDA, *page 118.*
DAWN CANADA: DisAbled Women's Network Canada;
Vancouver, British Columbia, 1988.

TRISHA MIFFLEN, *page 28.*
With Joshua and Liam; Single Mother; Antigonish,
Nova Scotia,1985.

ANGELA MILES, *page 154.*
Feminist Theorist, Educator; Toronto, Ontario;
photographed in 1977.

LISE MOISAN, *page 144.*
Lesbian-Feminist Activist; Montreal, Quebec, 1989.

THE MONTREAL ASSAULT PREVENTION CENTRE, *page 30.*
Lisa Weintraub and Leona Heillig; Montreal, Quebec, 1989.

SKY BLUE MARY MORIN, *page 92.*
With Raine; Native Activist, Spiritual Teacher;
Saskatoon, Saskatchewan, 1986.

JANE MORRIGAN, *page 20.*
Dairy Farmer; Scotsburn, Nova Scotia,1985.

MUMS, *page 44.*
Mothers United For Metro Shelter; Halifax, Nova Scotia, 1985.

CINDY MURRAY, *page 88.*
Farmer; Erickson, Manitoba, 1985.

NELLIE'S HOSTEL FOR WOMEN, *page 48.*
Heljo Liitoja, Margaret Moores, Leslie McDonald,
Carmen Bourbonnais, Diana Capponi, Nalini Singh,
Anne Elliott, Joyce Brown, Donna Wilson, Joan Headley;
Toronto, Ontario, 1984.

NORTHERN LIGHTS RESOURCE ASSOCIATION
AND CRISIS LINE, *page 32.* Hannah Murphy, Theresa Whitson,
Bea Kine; Westlock, Alberta, 1988.

MARY O'BRIEN, *page112.*
Philosopher, Theorist; Toronto, Ontario, 1981.

MADELEINE PARENT, *page 90.*
Feminist and Union Organizer; Montreal, Quebec, 1991.

THE PICTOU COUNTY WOMEN'S CENTRE, *page 56.*
Mary Petty, Dian Day, Coreen Popowich, Alexandra Keir,
Joanne Kohout, Judy Hughes, Jan Post Lewis, Donna
Mulrooney-Makhan (with Liam), Judy Schuhlein, Pat Smyth;
New Glasgow, Nova Scotia, 1985.

LE POINT DE RALLIEMENT DES FEMMES HAITIENNES
(Rallying Point for Haitian Women), *page 140.*

Josette Jean-Pierre Rousseau, Marlène Rateau, Aliette Saint-Jean,
Edna Etienne, Rose-Marie Gautier; Montreal, Quebec, 1989.

HELEN FOGWILL PORTER, *page 146.*
Writer, Activist; St John's, Newfoundland, 1986.

POWER, *page 108.*
Prostitutes and Other Women for Equal Rights;
"Kitten Blue"and Marie Arrington; Vancouver,
British Columbia, 1988.

KRIS PURDY AND HEATHER BISHOP, *page 76.*
Musicians, Singer-songwriters; Winnipeg, Manitoba, 1985.

THE QUEBEC IMMIGRANT WOMEN'S COLLECTIVE, *page 116.*
Elizabeth de Peslovan, Celina Hasbón, Homa Monfared, Aoura Bizzarri,
Blas Genao, Augustine Gonzalez; Montreal, Quebec, 1988.

THE RAGING GRANNIES, *page 128.*
Ruth Brown, Linda Siegel, Joyce Stewart, Bess Ready, Fran
Thoburn, Betty Brightwell, Hilda Marczak; Peace and
Environment Activists; Victoria, British Columbia, 1988.

REGINA TRANSITION WOMEN'S SOCIETY, *page 148.*
Candy Panzer, Deanna Elias-Henry, Louise Murray;
Regina, Saskatchewan, 1986.

JILLIAN RIDINGTON, *page 42.*
Former Chairperson, The BC Periodical Review Board;
Vancouver, British Columbia, 1988.

ANITA ROBERTS, *page 136.*
Assault Prevention Teacher; Vancouver, British Columbia, 1988.

ESTHER SHANNON, *page 70.*
Journalist, Former Editor of *Kinesis;* Vancouver,
British Columbia, 1988.

HARRIET AND SHIRLEY SIMAND, *page 98.*
Founders of DES Action Canada; Montreal, Quebec, 1989.

SOUTH ASIAN WOMEN'S COMMUNITY CENTRE, *Page 26.*
Sanjukta Dasgupta, Sabitri Ganguly, Regina Fernando,
Grace Gomez, Vanessa Chio; Montreal, Quebec,1989.

LESLIE SPILLETT, *page 102.*
Labour Activist; Winnipeg, Manitoba, 1985.

TAMARACK AND MOUNTAIN, *page 130.*
Founders of The Healing Centre for Women; Ottawa, Ontario, 1986.

MAXINE TYNES, *page 18.*
Poet; Dartmouth, Nova Scotia,1985.
"Womanskin" from *Borrowed Beauty,* Pottersfield Press,
Porter's Lake, NS, 1987, reprinted with permission.

ELIZABETH CUSACK WALSH, *page 46.*
Lawyer; Sydney, Nova Scotia, 1985.

WENDY WILLIAMS, *page 100.*
President, Provincial Council on the Status of Women;
St. John's, Newfoundland, 1986.

WOMEN'S SUPPORT GROUP, *page 164.*
Lorna Gallant, Beth Brehaut, Julie Dodd, Shirley Limbert, and
friends; Crowbush, Prince Edward Island, 1986.

MARIAN YEO, *page 40.*
Activist, Art Critic; Winnipeg, Manitoba, 1985.

EVE ZAREMBA, *page 110.*
Writer, Publisher, Toronto, Ontario, 1988.

BIOGRAPHICAL NOTES

PAMELA HARRIS is a photographer and writer best known for her portraits and extensive documentary work. She has recorded many different kinds of communities, including villages in the high arctic and in Newfoundland, migrant farmworkers and their union, her own extended family, and the feminist community in Canada. She is the author of *Another Way of Being*, photographs and writing from Spence Bay, Northwest Territories. In the early seventies she helped organize the first exhibition in Canada of photographs by and about women, and she produced *The Women's Kit*, a multi-media package for high schools. Her photographic work has been published and exhibited across North America for the past twenty-five years and is represented in many permanent collections. She has taught photography at the University of California at Santa Cruz and the Ontario College of Art. In 1990 she was the recipient of the Duke and Duchess of York Prize in Photography, awarded annually by the Canada Council.

ANGELA MILES has been involved in the Canadian women's movement since the early seventies. She was a founding member of the Feminist Party of Canada and the Antigonish Women's Resource Centre in Nova Scotia. She is active in the Canadian Research Institute for the Advancement of Women and in Toronto Women for a Just and Healthy Planet. She has a doctorate in Political Science from the University of Toronto and teaches at the Ontario Institute for Studies in Education. Her numerous publications include *Feminism: from Pressure to Politics* and *Feminist Radicalism in the 1980s*.

LISA STEELE's photo, film and video works have been exhibited extensively, and she is a frequent writer on culture and art. She has taught at the Ontario College of Art since 1981. She was a founding publisher of FUSE Magazine and the co-founder of V Tape, an information service for independent video. Since 1983 she has worked exclusively in collaboration with Kim Tomczak. In 1989-90 their work was the subject of a major exhibition at the Art Gallery of Ontario. Their first feature is *Legal Memory*.